Strange Unsolved Mysteries
by Margaret Ronan

SCHOLASTIC INC.
New York Toronto London Auckland Sydney

Other books by the author available
from Scholastic Book Services . . .

FACES ON FILM
**ASTROLOGY AND OTHER OCCULT
 GAMES**
**THE SHADOW OVER INNSMOUTH
 AND OTHER STORIES OF HORROR
 BY H. P. LOVECRAFT (editor)**

ISBN 0-590-42017-8

12 11 10 9 8 7 6 5 4 3 2 1   8 9/8 0 1 2 3/9

Printed in the U.S.A.   01

A word to the reader . . .

Ghosts . . . Premonitions . . . Dreams that come true . . . Hexes and curses . . . Objects that move by some secret force . . . Places where Mother Nature fools you! All these things can be found in this book — and more. Everything you read here really happened to real people! They are true unsolved mysteries that have been witnessed and authenticated.

How can such things be? Trained investigators (parapsychologists) are working now in university laboratories to try to find out. And some of these investigators suggest that many of these inexplicable events might be explained with three letters — ESP.

ESP stands for extrasensory perception. With sensory perception, we perceive with our five known senses — sight, hearing, taste, touch, and smell. But extrasensory perception seems to enable people to perceive through thus far unknown senses of the mind.

To these parapsychologists there are four kinds of ESP:

Clairvoyance — the ability to know what is happening at a distance, at the time it is happening.

Precognition — the ability to know what is going to happen before it happens.

Telepathy — the ability to send messages mentally to another mind.

Psychokinesis — the ability to move objects by force of will, without touching them.

If you like your mysteries to have solutions, you may enjoy deciding which kind of ESP might be the answer to some of the enigmas in this book. A clairvoyant, for example, might be able to read a sealed letter while blindfolded. A touch of precognition might give you hunches that work out. Someone who didn't know he or she had the gift of psychokinesis might set off so-called poltergeist activities.

If, on the other hand, you prefer your mysteries to stay unsolved, you can take comfort in the fact that many scientists say there is no such thing as ESP. They claim that tests made by parapsychologists in laboratories are not reliable. Other scientists say if ESP proves to be real, we will have to have a whole new set of physical laws — that it would require such new laws to explain many of the mysteries in this book.

CONTENTS

Batman and Robin and ESP

                      They leap from tall building to tall building. They scramble over roofs and drop through skylights in pursuit of lawbreakers. No wonder criminals and reporters alike call Dave Greenberg and Bob Hantz Batman and Robin.

Greenberg and Hantz are two New York detectives who work as a team. In four years of togetherness, they have racked up a super record of 600 felony arrests with a conviction rate of 93 percent. In the course of their duties, Dave has saved Bob's life three times, and Bob has saved Dave's twice.

How do they do it? "Blame it all on ESP," says Dave (Batman) Greenberg.

According to Greenberg, the ESP started to work when he and Hantz graduated from the Police Academy and were assigned to the traffic unit.

"We discovered that we had the ability to look at a car, and somehow *know* whether or not it was stolen. We'd be on our way to work, and *bingo!* — we'd get that weird feeling, and by the time we checked in, we'd have made a couple of stolen car arrests!"

Dave and Bob were promoted to the rank of detective together, and commended by the Police Commissioner for their "imagination, effort, and bravery." Using their ESP, they teamed up in a spree of crime-busting. "Often without speaking a word, we'll both know at the same time that something wrong is going on that we'd better look into. We don't have to tell each other who to go after. It's like having one mind in two bodies," says Bob.

Dave agrees. "If I get into a bad corner, Bob knows even if he isn't near. He has an uncanny ability to find me when I need him, no matter where I am."

To show how this works, Greenberg once invited a reporter to make a test. Bob went into a telephone booth. The reporter took Greenberg blocks away to hide him.

"That reporter really tried to get lost with me, but he didn't have a chance. I concentrated, Bob concentrated — and then Bob found me in less than ten minutes!"

This mental hookup with his partner gives Dave extra confidence. "As long as Bob's on my side, I'm all right. Once I was in a car with drug pushers. I was trying to convince them that I was a crooked cop looking for a bribe, but they found my hidden tape recorder and were going to kill me. One guy had a knife at my throat, and the other had a gun stuck in the pit of my stomach. Then in my mind I heard Bob say, 'Hang on, I'm on my way.' A few minutes later he drove up, yanked open the car door, and dragged those guys out. He didn't know where I was, but he found me."

How does Hantz's built-in direction-finder work? "Concentration," he says. "You have to empty your mind, make it a blank. Then you concentrate hard on the person you're trying to reach. You can't let anything distract you."

One morning Bob Hantz felt he had to call Greenberg at his home. When Greenberg answered, Hantz said, "Are you OK? I got a feeling something was wrong."

"Thank God you did," he heard Greenberg say. "Five guys are hiding outside in my yard, waiting to get me. Come on the double!"

Bob and a squad car screamed to the rescue.

Thanks to *The Supercops*, a book and a movie about them, Greenberg and Hantz are now famous. But they are more interested in doing their job as detectives than in being celebrities. The big problem is that, thanks to *The Supercops*, their identity is known to too many people, and their lives are in greater danger.

"But why should we worry?" asks Greenberg. "As long as Bob and I are tuned in to each other, our luck holds."

Bob agrees. "If I should ever fail Dave, the psychic relationship between us would be broken. I don't intend to fail."

Yellow Blob of Texas

When spring 1973 rolled around in Garland, Texas, Mrs. Marie Harris expected to find flowers blooming in her backyard. But what she found there drove the thought of flowers right out of her mind.

"It was about as big as a platter at first, and pale yellow. It looked sort of foamy and creamy."

That's how Mrs. Garland described her unexpected backyard visitor, the Blob, to reporters. How the Blob got into her yard no one could even begin to guess. But one thing was certain. Mrs. Harris didn't want it there. She didn't know what it was, or where it came from, but she was determined to get rid of it.

Mrs. Harris armed herself with weed killer, and sprayed the Blob. It shuddered and began to pulsate. Then Mrs. Harris got a hoe and gave it a couple of whacks. The Blob bled red and purple fluids, but it stayed put.

For days Mrs. Harris waged war on the Blob. She tried to set fire to it, but the Blob wouldn't burn. She attacked it with a lawn mower — and it just seemed to flatten out a little. And all the time it was growing. In three weeks, it doubled its size and changed its color scheme. Now it was yellow on the outside and orange on the inside.

Firemen and police inspected the Blob, shook their heads, and went away. Neighbors and reporters stopped by to look it over. So did Dr. C. J. Alexopolous, a biologist from the University of Texas. He snipped off a bit of the Blob and took it away to examine.

Meanwhile the Texas sun blazed away, and the Blob began to turn a little brown around the edges. Was the sun wilting it? Mrs. Harris thought the Blob looked less robust than usual, so she decided to attack it once more. This time she used a spray containing nicotine. The Blob pulsated madly, then shriveled up and died.

A report came back from the University of Texas. Dr. Alexopolous thought that the Blob *might* have been some kind of fungus — but he couldn't say what kind. A fungus that pulsated when attacked, and then bled red and purple, was unfamiliar to him.

"If that thing was a fungus, it wasn't a fungus from Earth," said one of Mrs. Harris' neighbors. "I'd bet my last dime it was some kind of spore

11

from outer space. I just hope it never comes back!"

If the Blob was really a visitor from outer space, Texans in Aurora wouldn't be surprised. Aurora is a little town 40 miles from Garland, and some people there claim they got an interstellar tourist back in April 1897.

According to Texas newspapers of the time, a "cigar-shaped" spaceship crashed into an Aurora windmill "with a tremendous explosion." But that wasn't all. In the wreckage, they found what remained of the ship's pilot — a very small being who was obviously "not an inhabitant of this world."

"I remember my parents telling how the flying ship exploded, and the pilot was torn up and killed," recalls Mary Evans. "What was left of him was buried in the Aurora graveyard."

As time went on, the UFO and its pilot were more or less forgotten — until a reporter named Bill Case happened to read those old 1897 newspaper reports. Case works for the *Dallas Times Herald*, and he was looking for a scoop.

According to the old newspapers, the spaceship had broken up into pieces of an "unknown metal." If Case could find some of those pieces, he would have a tremendous story. He teamed up with a professional treasure hunter named Frank Kelley, and the two men went off to Aurora. There they started digging around the site of the UFO crash — now a chicken coop at the back of a service station.

Sure enough, their digging turned up pieces of metal that looked like nothing known on Earth. Kelley turned his metal detector on it, and the metal gave off strange signals. On a hunch, Kelley and Case took the detector to the Aurora graveyard. There they turned it on the grave of the UFO pilot — and back came the same strange signals.

Samples of the metal have been sent to North Texas University, where physicist Dr. Tom Gray is checking them out. Dr. Gray admits the metal fragments are "very interesting," but he isn't saying whether or not they come from another world.

"One of the metal chips is mostly iron with about 25 percent zinc," says Gray. "Now that wouldn't be unusual if it were stainless steel — but it's not. I don't know what it is."

Gray says another bit of metal, however, is more suspicious. It is zinc and has American threads machined in it. "Who knows what a spaceship is made of? But I don't think a spaceship would carry American-threaded zinc. We've got a lot more testing to do on this one. It arouses my curiosity."

Senior citizen Charlie Stephens of Aurora is certain the metal is not of this Earth. He was there when the strange ship crashed into the windmill. "Just as sure as I'm alive, something whizzed out of the sky and smashed into Judge Proctor's windmill."

And in 1897, as Mr. Stephens points out, there were no known *earthly* pilot-carrying, power-driven, heavier-than-air flying objects!

The Mystery of the
Empty House

A haze of heat lay over the Austrian hills outside Vienna on that July day in 1908. But Hans-Peter Storrer and his wife, Therese, scarcely seemed to notice the humid weather. They were excitedly and hopefully hunting for a house of their own.

For two years the young couple had been forced to share the cramped apartment of Therese's parents. But now at last they had saved enough money to buy their own home.

Seated beside her husband in their open car, Therese's eyes searched the streets of every village through which they passed. Perhaps here — or here — would be the place they had dreamed about.

Suddenly Therese clutched her husband's arm. "Look! A 'For Sale' sign. There, to the left, up that lane. I can see it through the trees."

Hans-Peter turned the car around and started up the lane. Sure enough, there was the sign, and beyond it on a little hill, the house.

As he brought the car to a stop in front of the entrance, it was plain to the young couple that the house had been empty for a long time. The garden was choked with weeds. Grass had sprouted in the driveway. The bricks of the house's walls were flaking, and the paint on the window frames and door peeling.

"Look!" said Therese in astonishment. "Someone is home. The curtain on that window moved. Whoever it is saw us drive up."

Hurriedly, the young people got out of the car and knocked on the door. They could hear the echoes of the knocker resounding inside. But no one came. "I must have been mistaken," Therese said. "But look through this window. You can see furniture inside."

Hans-Peter banged the knocker again. "If the owners have left furniture, they must also have left a caretaker," he said firmly.

His knocking went unanswered. Angrily, he tried the door and found it unlocked. At his push, it swung open. The young couple stepped inside, and stood transfixed with astonishment.

The furniture and curtains they had seen through the window were thickly covered with dust and cobwebs. In the dining room, a table had been set for a meal long ago — a meal

15

that only mice had eaten. In the kitchen and pantry, food was laid out. Some of it was coated now with mold, some had crumbled into dust.

Therese felt a stirring of panic. "I wanted to leave," she recalled later, "but Hans-Peter was determined to see all the rooms. He half-dragged me from floor to floor, but we found no one and nothing but dusty furniture. But when we returned to the ground floor, he stopped and pointed at the end of the gloomy corridor. 'We missed that room,' he said, 'perhaps the caretaker's hiding there.'

"He opened the big double doors to the room — and we saw *them!* There were people in there — a man, a woman, and two children. They were just sitting in chairs by the fireplace, looking at us. I could see that their clothes were very old-fashioned, like those of the 1880's.

"We just stood there, too astonished to move. The eyes of those four were the saddest I have ever seen."

The look exchanged by the Storrers and the four strangers lasted only a few minutes. Then, like a slow dissolve in a movie, the four faded away and vanished. The Storrers also vanished, running out of the house as fast as they could.

Back in Vienna, they told their friends about their strange experience. One friend urged them to return to the village. "Ghosts always have a reason for coming back," said the friend. "I think you should find out as much as you can about the history of the house."

Therese refused to go, but Hans-Peter took his friend's advice and drove back to the village some weeks later. Realizing that the man likely to know the most about the village would be the postmaster, he went directly to the post office.

"The house on the hill?" asked the postmaster. "It has been for sale for a long time now, but I doubt that anyone will ever buy it. No one has wanted to live there since the owner killed his wife and two children. Afterward, he shot himself. It was in the newspapers. See, I still have a copy."

The postmaster opened a drawer and drew out a yellowed newspaper. "Family Tragedy!" blared the headline. "Murder and Suicide!" But Hans-Peter needed to read no further. He was staring at the photograph beneath the headline — a photograph of the four people he and Therese had seen in the empty house.

The Phantom Porthole

At the quay in Cape Town, South Africa, the 38,000-ton liner *Windsor Castle* lay gleaming in the morning sun. The ship's officer who was making a routine inspection of the liner eyed her with satisfaction. Very shortly now, she would be embarking on her homeward voyage to Southampton, England.

Suddenly he uttered an exclamation of disgust. The glass of one of the portholes was filmed with dust and dirt. The officer hurriedly went aboard to scold the steward who had failed to clean the porthole.

When the steward was found, he seemed bewildered. "But there can't be a porthole there, sir," he protested. "There's no cabin in that part of the *Castle*."

"I'll see about that!" snapped the officer. "You come with me."

Together the two men checked out each cabin on the liner. In every one, the porthole was clean and shining. Puzzled, the officer went back to the quay. Yes, there it was — that dirt-encrusted porthole!

Angrily, the officer went back on board and ordered an able seaman lowered over the side on a rope to examine the mystery.

"There's a porthole there all right, sir," the man reported when he had been pulled back up on deck. "It's hard to see through all that dirt, but I looked in. I spied a double cabin in there, sir, with bunks, a chest of drawers, and a washbasin. But the funny thing was — I couldn't see a door!"

It was impossible to delay the *Castle*'s sailing, so the great liner went to sea with the double mystery of the dirty porthole and the doorless cabin still intact. But now the young officer was determined to find a solution. He ordered a full-scale search from deck to deck. Under his watchful eyes, all bulkheads and partitions were tapped from top to bottom.

On D Deck, his persistence paid off. "I think I've found it, sir," reported one of the crew. "There's a section of wall for'ard in the crew's quarters that sounds hollow."

The officer ordered the wall broken through. When an opening had been made, he found himself staring into a dusty cabin. Bunks, chest of drawers, washbasin — it was all as the seaman who had investigated the porthole on the rope had described. All, that is, except for the dirty porthole. There was no porthole!

The cabin had obviously been walled up soon after the ship was built, and that was why the seaman had seen no door. But what about the porthole? Where was it?

The disused cabin was boarded up and a guard posted. A man was again sent over the side to check on the porthole. It was still there, still dirty and dusty from the inside. But on looking through it, the man could not see any sign of the broken wall which had just been boarded up.

Rumors buzzed about the mystery porthole during the voyage until the Captain ordered them stopped. They broke out again, however, when the ship reached port. Soon the rumors reached the ears of local newspaper reporters, who crowded onto the ship.

"It's just sailors' gossip," said the Captain. "Not a word of truth in any of it, and I would advise you gentlemen not to print a word of this nonsense. There is no such mystery cabin on my ship. And if you can find a dirty porthole on this ship, I'll thank you to point it out to me."

The reporters looked, but the Captain was right. Every porthole was spick and span.

The member of the crew who told me about the phantom porthole offered this theory. "That porthole was there on the voyage, and it was gone when we docked. It will be back on every voyage. It's not really a porthole, you see. It's the ship's ghost."

Dogs with Human Brains

"Dumb animals," we say. Do we mean by "dumb" that animals can't talk, or do we mean that they are stupid? Used in either sense, the word "dumb" cannot apply to the dogs in this chapter. All showed almost human intelligence, and all could communicate their thoughts and opinions to humans.

Jim was an English setter, the pet of hotel-owner Sam Van Arsdale. For the first four years of Jim's life, he seemed to be just an ordinary dog. Then one day in 1929 he seemed to take several giant leaps up the IQ scale.

On that particular day, Van Arsdale was strolling around the hotel grounds with Jim. A variety of trees grew there, and one of them caught Van Arsdale's attention.

"That elm over there looks like it's got some kind of blight," he said to himself. "I wonder if any of the other elms have caught it."

To Van Arsdale's amazement, Jim broke away from his side. The dog scampered across the lawn to another elm, and came to a halt at the foot of the tree, whining and barking. When Van Arsdale examined the tree, he discovered it too had the beginnings of a blight disease also. But how had Jim known what Van Arsdale was talking about, and how had he known which tree to find?

Was it just coincidence, wondered Van Arsdale — or could it be that Jim actually knew one tree from another? Aloud he murmured, "Find a birch tree, Jim."

Obediently, Jim ran off, coming to a halt in front of a birch. Astonished, Van Arsdale forgot about coincidence, and began to test the dog. Could Jim pick out a locust tree, an oak, a beech? The dog could and did. Further experiments showed he could also tell one make of car from another.

Jim, it soon developed, had another talent — one which made him famous and made other people money. Van Arsdale discovered that Jim could pick the winners of horse races. He would read the names of horses scheduled to run in an upcoming race, and Jim would bark when the name of the winner was read out. When the race was run, the horse that Jim had chosen never failed to come in first.

Jim could also pick winners if Van Arsdale wrote the names of the horses on slips of paper. When the slips were laid on the floor in front of the dog, he would look them over, then place his paw on his choice. Crowds came to see Jim do this trick, then many of them would rush off to place their bets. Van Arsdale, however, never bet on Jim's tips. He didn't believe in gambling.

As might be expected, Jim became a celebrity. A movie company offered to star him, but Van Arsdale said no. Thinking Van Arsdale must have some secret set of signals that he passed along to Jim, Professors Durant and Dickinson of the University of Missouri asked if they might test him — without Van Arsdale. Jim was taken to the university to perform before an audience of 900 spectators. Although Jim had never heard anything but English spoken, he had no trouble carrying out orders given him in German, Spanish, and Italian!

Jim's ability to understand foreign languages, however, was only part of the show. Next the professors ordered him to go down into the audience.

"Look around and find a man with a black moustache," they told the dog. Without hesitating, Jim located such a man and placed his paw on the gentleman's knee. "Find a lady in a blue dress." Jim did so after a few minutes of searching. "Now, find a little girl wearing white stockings." This took a little longer, but Jim finally turned up a child answering that description.

The professors were impressed with Jim's abilities, and so was the Missouri state legislature. They suspended government business for a day so that Jim could perform for them. The legislators rigged up a test they felt sure Jim wouldn't be able to pass. They hired a telegrapher to tap out instructions to the dog in Morse code. Surely Jim would be confused by dots and dashes.

But the code was no riddle to Jim. When the telegrapher tapped out instructions to find a certain senator, Jim made a beeline for the right man. The legislature gave the dog a standing ovation.

As the years went by, Jim became feeble and seemed less interested in performing for curious humans. But in 1936 an election of national importance was to be held. To settle arguments among his friends, Van Arsdale asked Jim to predict the winner — the man who would be elected President of the United States. *The Reader's Digest* had predicted that Alfred Landon, the Republican candidate, would occupy the White House.

Jim disagreed. His choice was Franklin D. Roosevelt — by a landslide. But this was his last prediction, and like all the others he made, it was right on target.

Was Jim psychic? Did he read the minds of those humans who plagued him with questions? If so, this would account for his uncanny ability to understand any language and code. There seems to be no other explanation.

There is even less explanation for the case of the speaking dog. Two men in Pittsburgh swore they met such a dog on July 29, 1908.

The men were out for a walk on Lincoln Avenue. An ordinary black dog trotted up to them, wagging its tail.

"Good morning," said the dog.

Aghast, the men looked at each other. Was one of them a ventriloquist, playing a joke?

"Not at all," said the dog. "I speak for myself."

With that the dog went on its way. Stunned and speechless, the men watched. Then one of them suddenly became angry.

"It's a trick!" he shouted. "Let's grab that animal and find out how it's done."

Leaving his friend, he ran after the dog. What happened next was reported to the policeman on the beat by his friend. The man who had chased the dog was too hysterical to make sense.

"He chased the dog, officer, and caught up with it. He was going to grab it when the creature said, 'Don't touch me!' But he did, anyway — caught hold of one of its legs. Then he let out a terrible scream! The dog got away. But look at my poor friend's hand!"

He pried open the clenched fingers of the hysterical man's hand. A livid mark, patterned with an etching of dog hairs, was burned into the palm.

The last word in stories about weird and wonderful dogs belongs to Chris, owned by George Wood of Rhode Island. Just for fun, in 1953 Mr. Wood decided to teach Chris to count by saying numbers out loud, then tapping the dog's paw on the chair a corresponding number of times.

Chris proved to be an astoundingly quick pupil. In almost no time at all, he learned to count up to a million, and then went on to learn addition, subtraction, and cube root problems. He also learned to spell by putting his paw on cards marked with letters of the alphabet.

Like Jim's, Chris's fame soon spread. And like Jim, he became the subject of a number of scientific tests. Research specialists from universities in Rhode Island, South Carolina, and Delaware put him through his paces.

For one test, the scientists thought up a problem so complicated that they believed only a computer could solve it. Chris came up with the correct answer in — *four minutes!*

"How did he do it?" the specialists asked each other.

"Smart dog," Chris spelled out with his alphabet cards. "Brain power!"

The Curse of
Rudolph Valentino's Ring

Do some objects have a mysterious, terrible power to bring harm to their owners? Can there be any basis of fact in the belief that a jewel can carry a curse, or a ring bring death?

The famous people who owned a certain silver ring might have once had answers to these questions. But we can't ask them what they think now, for they are all dead.

The story of the silver ring begins in San Francisco in 1920 in a certain jewelry store. Movie stars from Hollywood seldom visited the shop. Therefore the proprietor was astonished to see Rudolph Valentino, a superstar of the day, gazing at the display in the store's window.

He would have been even more astonished if

he had realized that Valentino was looking with complete fascination at a rather nondescript ring. He had been about to pass the jewelry store without a glance when the ring caught his eye.

It was not a very costly ring. It was not even beautiful, with its plain silver setting and odd semiprecious stone. But Valentino knew he must have it. He insisted on buying it even though the proprietor tried to discourage him.

"The ring has an evil history. Some say it even has a curse on it. All who have owned it died very soon after buying it, I am told," the proprietor warned.

Valentino scarcely seemed to listen. He bought the ring and seemed to enjoy telling his friends about its so-called curse. It was a good story, so the publicity department of his studio urged him to wear it in his next film, *The Young Rajah*. Was it Valentino's fault — or the ring's — that the movie was his first big flop?

Valentino certainly didn't seem to think it was the fault of the ring. He wore it in his next — and last — film, *The Son of the Sheik*. He was still wearing it when he went on a vacation trip to New York City. It was on his finger when he died three weeks later of acute appendicitis.

The ring next became the property of another well-known movie star of the 1920's, Pola Negri. She received the ring as a memento of her friendship with Valentino. But Pola found her luck turning bad as soon as she put the ring on her finger. She became ill and was sick for almost a year. When she finally recovered, she discovered that her fans had forgotten her, and her career was over.

Miss Negri never said whether she blamed the ring, but she got rid of it. At a party she noticed a young man who reminded her of her dead friend, Rudolph Valentino. She introduced herself, and learned that he was a popular singer named Russ Colombo.

"You must have this ring," said Pola Negri to Colombo. She handed it to him. "Let us say it is from one Valentino to another."

Colombo wore the ring, but not for long. Shortly afterward, he was killed in a shooting accident.

The ring, however, was still around. Now it belonged to Joe Casino, a friend of Colombo's. Perhaps Casino felt unhappy vibrations from the ring. At any rate, he put it into a glass case instead of wearing it. But one day he forgot to be careful. He took the ring out and put it on his hand. A week later he died in a traffic accident.

Joe Casino died wearing the ring, but it was not buried with him. His brother, Del Casino, took it. Del told everyone that he didn't believe in curses. "The only way to chase spooks is to laugh at them!" he would say.

Time passed, and Del still wore the ring, happily and proudly. Had his common sense killed off the curse? That's the way it seemed until Del put the ring into a safe in his home. Shortly afterward, a burglar named James Willis broke into the Casino house. The burglar alarm went off, bringing police cars screaming to the scene. A shot was fired, killing Willis. In his pocket the police found Valentino's ring.

The ring went back into the safe, and might have stayed there harmlessly. Then producer Edward Small decided to make a movie about the great Valentino. He sent out a call for a Valentino look-alike. He found one — a 21-year-old skater named Jack Dunn.

Dunn resembled Valentino so closely that the two men could have been twins. But could he act? A screen test would tell. For the test, Small had Dunn dress in some of Valentino's clothes. He also borrowed the ring from Del Casino so that Dunn could wear it.

The test was a great success. But ten days later, Jack Dunn died of a rare blood disease.

Casino reclaimed the ring. No one, he swore, would ever wear it again. It went into a safe deposit box in a Los Angeles bank. But even the steel walls of the safe deposit vault can't seem to contain the ring's evil influence. Robberies, strikes, and a fire have all come to the bank since the ring was put there.

A Dream of Disaster

On the night of July 3, 1944, Mrs. Amy Bond woke shuddering from an eerily vivid dream. Every detail stood out clearly in her mind.

"I seemed to be suspended in space above an island in the Pacific. I could see a long sweep of beach below me. To the right of the beach were some scrubby-looking trees, under which some Marines crouched. I recognized one of the Marines as my son. He was aiming up toward a hill beyond him with a thing that looked like a long pipe."

As Mrs. Bond watched in her dream, she could see enemy guns firing down on the Marines from the hill. She could also see other Marines crawling through what seemed to be high grass "with sticks protruding above leaves." She got the impression that the crawling Marines were trying to get up the hill.

"Then I saw two Marines coming down the hill, carrying someone on a stretcher. The man on the stretcher was covered by a blanket. When the Marines got to where my son was standing beneath the trees, they put the stretcher down on the ground beside him. I could see my son talking to them.

"Suddenly the top of the hill seemed to explode in flames. Smoke poured out, and pieces of metal rained down. Everything was enveloped in flames! The weapon my son had been using was torn to bits. He now lay on the ground, and there seemed to be something terribly wrong with his arms and legs. His eyes were closed, and his face was blackened, but he was still breathing.

"I was screaming and trying to get close enough to do something for him, but I couldn't seem to reach the beach. The person on the stretcher was still now, and I knew he was dead. It was not given to me to see what else happened. The dream ended, and I woke up."

The dream haunted Mrs. Bond all day. It could so easily have been true. World War II was raging and her son *was* a Marine, serving in the South Pacific. He could easily have been landed on one of those islands still held by the Japanese forces.

Later in the day Mrs. Bond received a letter from her son. He wrote that he was well, but she did not feel reassured. She put off going to bed until late, afraid she might again have the nightmare.

"The last time I looked at the clock, it was

three A.M. Shortly before five in the morning, I woke in a cold sweat. I had dreamed the whole horrible thing again. It was so etched on my mind that I got out of bed and made a sketch of what I had seen."

By the morning of July fifth, Mrs. Bond was convinced that what she had dreamed twice had actually happened — thousands of miles away in the South Pacific. Again that night she postponed falling asleep as long as she could. Again she dreamed the dreaded dream.

"When I awoke, I decided to write my daughter-in-law. I wrote that my son had been wounded, and that she would soon hear from the Navy. I told her not to worry because the wound would not be fatal."

The message that Mrs. Bond had predicted came to her daughter-in-law weeks later. It said that her husband had been wounded, and was recuperating on the hospital ship *Comfort*. Then came a message from Mrs. Bond's son: "Got hurt, but not bad enough to come home."

Mrs. Bond realized that on July third, fourth, and fifth, she had been dreaming of the future. At that time, the Navy was planning to invade the Japanese-held island of Guam. Mrs. Bond's son was one of the Marines who made the first landing — and one of those to be badly wounded.

When the war was over, and her son was home again, Mrs. Bond showed him a sketch she had made of her dream. He shook his head in astonishment and said, "If I didn't know better, I'd swear you made this drawing right on the scene. It's as accurate as if you were there."

What Mrs. Bond had sketched was the beach at Guam. The grass with "sticks protruding above leaves" was a sugarcane field through which the Marines crawled to try to reach the fortified hill.

"But who was the man on the stretcher?" Mrs. Dean wondered.

"Pfc. Thompson," her son replied. "He shouldn't have been in the battle at all. The commanding officer had just found out he was only sixteen, and was going to send him back to the States. But he never made it. He died there on the beach when the guns blew up. There's something terrible about a kid like Thompson getting killed on an island six thousand miles from home!"

Mrs. Bond understood how her son felt. She too had seen Pfc. Thompson die.

When Abraham Lincoln Spoke with Spooks

In the Library of Congress in Washington, D. C., these words are a matter of record:

"For more than an hour, I was made to talk to Mr. Lincoln. I learned from my friends afterward that it was upon matters that he seemed fully to understand, while they comprehended very little until the portion was reached that related to the forthcoming Emancipation Proclamation."

The words are those of Nettie Colburn, the so-called "child medium" who became famous as a psychic in Washington, D. C., in the mid-1800's.

Many Washingtonians came to watch Nettie go into trances during which she was believed to be talking with spirits. Among the spectators was Mary Todd Lincoln, wife of the President of the United States.

Mrs. Lincoln was worried about her husband. The President was bowed down by the defeats of Union troops in 1862, and by the controversy over his plans for an Emancipation Proclamation.

Perhaps, thought Mrs. Lincoln, Nettie Colburn could offer the President comfort and advice.

In December 1862 Mrs. Lincoln invited Nettie to come to the "Red Parlor" in the White House.

"The President stood before me," Nettie recalled later, "with a smile on his face. Dropping his hand upon my head, he said in a humorous tone, 'So this is our little Nettie, that we have heard so much about.' "

Nettie was then seated in a high-backed chair. Her eyes closed, and she slipped into a deep trance. There was silence for a time, and then she began to speak. But the voice that came from her lips was a man's, rich and deep.

"The war will never cease, the shouts of victory will never ring through the North until you issue the proclamation that shall set free the enslaved millions of your unhappy country," said the strange voice.

There was a breathless pause, and then the voice continued. "Stand firm upon your convictions. It is your duty to fearlessly perform the work, and fulfill the mission for which you have been raised up by Providence. Do not compromise the terms of the Emancipation Proclamation! You must not delay the enforcement of the proclamation beyond the first of the year."

When Nettie regained consciousness, she found herself surrounded by grave faces. Dazed, she knew nothing that had happened during her trance. She saw the President looking at her with a strained expression.

"Did the voice we heard not have a familiar sound to you, sir?" asked one of the men present.

The President nodded and glanced at the portrait of Daniel Webster, hanging on the wall. "Yes, and it is very singular," he said thoughtfully. "Miss Colburn, you have a remarkable gift."

Abraham Lincoln seemed to take seriously the advice that he received at Nettie's seance. He issued the Emancipation Proclamation on January 1, 1863. Later, when Nettie's spirit voices advised him to improve the morale of the soldiers by visiting their camps, he did so.

Nettie was not the only medium that the President consulted during the anguish of the Civil War. He also invited a medium named J. B. Conklin to conduct seances at the White House on four succeeding Sundays. Mr. Conklin not only served up messages from the spirit world. According to witnesses, he also caused a piano to rise several inches from the floor by itself, even though several spectators tried to hold it down.

Many people did not approve of the President's habit of holding seances at the White House. Newspapers often printed articles scolding Lincoln for "consulting spooks." But Lincoln paid no heed. Such articles, he felt, were written by people who could "not begin to tell the wonderful things I have witnessed."

Years later, Nettie Colburn wrote a book called *Was Abraham Lincoln a Spiritualist?* Like many people of his time, he seems to have accepted the central teaching of Spiritualism, that the spirit lives on after death.

"Mr. Lincoln was deeply interested in the great mysteries," Nettie wrote in answer to the question posed by her book's title. "But because he never openly committed himself, it is impossible to say whether or not Mr. Lincoln was a spiritualist."

Lincoln himself seems to have been gifted with ESP. He often had dreams that foretold the future. The most famous of these dreams is on record, for he told it to many friends.

"There seemed to be a deathlike stillness about me," he said. "Then I heard sobs, as if a number of people were weeping. I left my bed and wandered downstairs. There the silence was broken by the same pitiful sobbing, but the mourners were invisible. I went from room to room. No living person was in sight, but the same mournful sounds of distress met me as I passed along.

"It was light in all the rooms. Every object was familiar to me. But where were all the people who were grieving as if their hearts would break? I was puzzled and alarmed. What could be the meaning of all this? Determined to find the cause of things so mysterious and so shocking, I kept on until I arrived at the East Room, which I entered. There I met with a sickening surprise. Before me lay a corpse wrapped in funeral vestments. Around it were stationed soldiers who were acting as guards; and there was a throng of people, some gazing upon the corpse whose face was covered, others weeping pitifully.

" 'Who is dead in the White House?' I demanded of one of the soldiers.

" 'The President,' was his answer. 'He was killed by an assassin.'

"Then came a loud burst of grief from the crowd, which awoke me from my dream. I slept no more that night, and although it was only a dream, I have been strangely anxious about it ever since."

On April 7, 1865, two days before the Confederate General, Robert E. Lee, surrendered to General Grant of the Union forces — Lincoln had another dream that troubled him greatly.

"I seemed to be on a deep broad rolling river. I was in a boat, and I was falling in! Falling in!"

On the next two nights, Lincoln had this same dream again. It left him depressed and anxious. On the morning of his death, he told Senator Charles Sumner, "I know something extraordinary is about to happen, and very soon."

That night, as he sat with his wife in Ford's Theater, Lincoln was shot to death by John

39

Wilkes Booth. His dreams of impending doom had come true.

But this is not the end of the story. Although the Great Emancipator has been dead for over one hundred years, many people say his ghost still haunts the White House. According to one report, he paid a courtesy call when Queen Wilhelmina of Holland visited President Franklin D. Roosevelt at the Executive Mansion. The Queen heard a knock at the door of her suite. When she opened it, there stood Lincoln smiling down upon her with a twinkle in his eyes. Then he was gone — but not before she got the impression that the 16th U.S. President was indeed in the best of spirits!

The Voice from Nowhere

Fog . . .

It spread a veil over Monterey and muffled
Richard Bach's footsteps as he strode along.

Bach walked rapidly through the quiet
streets. Perhaps he was trying to outstrip his
troubles, but they kept pace with him. For one
thing, he was broke and without a job. He had
been trained as an Air Force pilot, but no one
in private industry seemed to want to pay him
to fly. Now he was trying to eke out a living for
his family by writing aviation articles for maga-
zines. Between articles he did odd jobs — sometimes selling jewelry, sometimes delivering telephone books. No one asked Bach what he really
wanted to do, but if they had he would have
answered: "Fly!"

He had reached a canal near the beach when
the voice spoke to him. It came out of thin air,
and it said:

"Jonathan Livingstone Seagull!"

Bach spun around. He could see no one. He stared wildly around. Had he really heard those words? What did they mean?

Was he dreaming? No, he told himself, that voice was real. He hurried home and went to his room. A voice had spoken to him. Now he would speak to it.

"Look, voice," he said out loud. "If you think I know what this means, you're out of your mind. But if it means something, tell me."

What happened next sent Bach rushing to his desk to grab up paper and a ballpoint pen. A strange vision was flooding through his mind — a vision that seemed almost like a 3-D movie. "I realized at once that I was supposed to write it down, not just watch it," he recalls now. And what he saw and wrote turned out to be the first part of a best seller-to-be, *Jonathan Livingstone Seagull*.

Suddenly the vision stopped — just at the point where Jonathan is cast out by his flock. Bach was desperate. "It was just like watching a screen go blank. For weeks I tried to figure out what came next. I just couldn't think of a way to end the story."

The weeks grew into months, and then into eight years. Bach moved from California to Ottumwa, Iowa. He was still writing aviation articles. And since flight and birds went together in his mind, he wrote an article about sea gulls. In this article, he said that gulls could and should improve their flying skills.

Perhaps it was the effect of the sea gull article,

but one night in 1967 Bach had a strange dream about sea gulls. He woke up suddenly, his mind filled with pictures. The vision was back, and the further adventures of Jonathan Livingstone Seagull seemed to be unreeling before his eyes.

"That strange visionesque thing picked up just where it left off in Monterey," says Bach, "and there was the end of the story. I jumped out of bed and started putting it down — this time on an electric typewriter."

Once down on paper, *Jonathan Livingstone Seagull* went on to become a best-selling book and a movie. But even today, Bach feels he was only the recorder — not the true author of the story. "I don't even write in that style," he points out. When readers ask him what the book really means, Bach replies that he doesn't know. "If I had really originated the book myself, I could say what it meant. But I didn't, so I can't."

Who was the real author of *Jonathan Livingstone Seagull*? Whose voice spoke to Richard Bach out of the fog? No one knows the answers to these questions, but here's an odd coincidence. Back in the 1930's, there was a racing pilot and aircraft designer named John Livingstone. His clipped-wing cabin Monocoupe whizzed past plenty of pylons.

What has a pilot named Jonathan Livingstone got to do with an imaginary sea gull named Jonathan Livingstone?

Draw your own conclusions.

Wrong-Way Places

_____

Joshua Marcy pulled the reins, halting his horse. The animal's sides were heaving, and its breathing was strained.

"Anyone would think you were climbing this hill — not walking down it," Joshua muttered in bewilderment. He dismounted and began to lead the horse downhill, only to have the mystery deepen!

The further down man and horse walked, the more labored grew the horse's breathing. And by the time they reached the bottom of the hill, Joshua found himself tired, out of breath, and baffled!

What ailed Joshua and his horse? Nothing at all. Their only problem was that they were on Spook Hill, one of the eeriest places in the world. Spook Hill is located in Central Florida, and on it gravity seems upside down. Going up Spook Hill takes no effort at all. But going downhill, as Joshua and his horse discovered, takes real stamina.

No one knows why Spook Hill behaves this way. Some people claim the place is bewitched, cursed by a long-dead Indian chief. But whatever the cause, Spook Hill is spooky! Just ask any of the thousands of tourists who visit it each year. To test Spook Hill's wayward ways, they can park their cars at the bottom — putting the cars in neutral with the brakes off. Then, slowly but surely, the cars will back up the hill all by themselves!

Joshua probably couldn't have even coaxed his horse near another wrong-way place — the Oregon Vortex. Horses tend to shy away from the Vortex, and so do birds. You can hear birds in the forest beyond, but try to find a single one in the area of the Vortex. Most people say that the first time they enter the Vortex, they feel like imitating the birds and going somewhere else.

The Oregon Vortex is at Gold Hill, not too far from Grant's Pass in Oregon. It's a circle about 165 feet in diameter. Right at the heart of the circle is the "House of Mystery," a crazily tilted wooden shack.

Back in the 1880's, the shack was an assay office where gold was brought to be weighed. At that time, it is said that the shack stood on *top* of the hill! Then strange things began to happen. The scales used in weighing ore stopped working properly. How could they, when the pans of the balance had a tendency to tilt toward the magnetic north instead of hanging straight down?

The assay office was closed down — but not before people noticed another strange thing: The shack was *moving!* Slowly it seemed to be creeping down the hill toward the vortex, almost as if it were being pulled.

The Indians in the area weren't a bit surprised at these goings-on. They had always kept their distance from the Vortex. They noticed that the trees which grew within the circle did not stand up straight, but tended to lean to the north. They knew the place was uncanny, and called it the Forbidden Ground.

Today the Oregon Vortex is a tourist attraction. Visitors from all over the world come to test its strange powers. Once inside the "House of Mystery," as the old assay shack is now called, they find themselves leaning at an angle of ten degrees toward the center of the circle. If they try to balance themselves by leaning backward, they seem to feel a strong pull from the center of the circle.

Is this feeling of being pulled imaginary? Many scientific investigators say no. They have measured an unusually strong gravitational pull at the center of the Vortex. They say that the Vortex is a kind of "whirlpool of force."

If you have trouble imagining a "whirlpool of force," think of the Vortex as a huge ball, half buried in the ground. The ball would contain the strong force. Anything entering the area of the ball would feel that force.

Investigators don't know why the Vortex works the way it does, but they have conducted a number of experiments to try to find out. In one experiment, a 28-pound steel ball was hung on a chain from one of the shack's roof beams. This ball is still there, and it hangs at a ten degree angle, as if it were reaching for the center of the circle. You can shove it so it hangs straight down, but it won't stay that way.

If you visit the Vortex, you can test its power in a number of ways. Place a ball or an empty glass jar on a sloping board in the shack, and these objects will roll *uphill!* A rubber ball placed on the outer edge of the Vortex will roll toward the center. You can get sticks or brooms or golf clubs to stand on end on the edge of the Vortex circle — if you lean them at a ten degree angle away from the circle's center. You can get a broom to stand upright on a sloping board.

In the strange world of the Vortex, you will appear much shorter when you face south, and taller when you face north. If another person walks away from you toward the south, he will seem to become taller. But if he walks toward you from the same direction, he will appear to become shorter! But you'll have to know which is north or south without a compass. In the Oregon Vortex, compasses just don't work.

The Brooklyn Enigma

An enigma is a puzzle, a mystery for which there is no explanation. There are human enigmas, and Mollie Fancher was one of them. Many people witnessed her strange powers, but no one could explain how she did what she did.

To those who didn't know her, Mollie seemed an object of pity. Born in 1858, she suffered serious accidents at 18 that left her blind and bedridden for the remaining thirty years of her life. She could not even sit up in bed, for her legs were twisted under her, and her right arm was locked for many years behind her head. Nevertheless, the people who came in contact with Mollie soon ceased to feel sorry for her. This seemingly helpless woman had abilities they could not begin to understand.

For one thing Mollie could *see* although she

was blind. Said her personal physician, Dr. S. F. Speir, "She can perceive anything placed on her forehead or on the top of her head!" With other physicians as witnesses, Dr. Speir often watched Mollie do crochet or embroidery work by holding the work at the *back of her head.*

"When she chooses different colors for the embroidery, she puts the embroidery silks behind her head and names the colors. Although her right arm is locked in a paralyzed position behind her head, Mollie works by bringing her left hand back to the right hand."

To make sure there was no trickery, Dr. Speir called in oculists to examine Mollie's eyes. These specialists all agreed that she was indeed blind. Incredible! thought Dr. Speir, and he dreamed up another test for his patient. He had bits of cloth, each of a different color, in his pocket. Then he asked Mollie to name the color of each piece he touched. Mollie named every color correctly.

One of Mollie's closest friends was the distinguished New York judge, Abram H. Dailey. Judge Dailey wrote a book about Mollie entitled *Mollie Fancher: The Brooklyn Enigma.* In it he reported other incidents which proved that Mollie did not need eyes to see.

A letter came to Mollie through the mail, and her sister offered to read it to her. Mollie shook her head. She took up a piece of chalk with her left hand and wrote on a slate: "No, I will read it."

According to Dr. Ormiston, a friend of Dr.

Speir's, the letter was still sealed in its envelope. Nevertheless, "Miss Fancher proceeded to write out, word for word, every sentence in the letter. When I opened the letter and read it aloud myself, it was the same as the message Miss Fancher had written."

Judge Dailey was not at all surprised at this. "She has read sealed letters which were placed on her forehead. She has done so hundreds of times to my knowledge."

However, one day Judge Dailey did get a surprise. When he visited Mollie, she told him that she had been at his house the night before.

"How can that be?" he asked. "We both know you cannot leave this bed."

Mollie smiled, and then described perfectly the room she claimed to have visited in the judge's house. "A man was visiting you there at the time," she said. "A tall thin man with a dark complexion."

The judge did not say so, but he knew Mollie was right. The previous night he had entertained a Mr. Sisson, and Mollie's description fitted Sisson perfectly. But here, the judge realized, was an opportunity for another test of Mollie's remarkable abilities.

A few days later, he brought two men with him when he visited Mollie. One of them was Sisson, but the identity of both was carefully kept from the blind woman.

"Do you know either of the gentlemen with me?" he asked Mollie.

"They have never been here before," replied Mollie, "but one of them is the man with the dark complexion I saw at your house." And she raised her left hand to point at Sisson.

Another secret test for Mollie was dreamed up by a man named Louis Sherk. He hired a man to go to the Fancher house in Brooklyn to hang a picture in the front room. "I told him where to hang it if he found no one in the room. The folding doors between the front and back rooms were closed. Mollie of course was upstairs in bed. She did not know the man was coming."

As the man began to hammer a picture hook into the wall, a woman's voice spoke crossly behind him.

"No, not there, you fool. On the opposite wall, where the light is better."

Startled, the man whirled around. No one else was in the room. He shook his head, and began to hammer once more.

"I told you — not there!" shouted the voice.

Thoroughly frightened, the man left the house. "I wouldn't go back there for any amount of money," he told Sherk. "The devil must live there!"

"No devil spoke to you," replied Sherk, laughing. "The voice you heard belongs to Mollie Fancher. Although she is blind and paralyzed, she can evidently see through walls!"

In her later years, Mollie not only seemed to be able to see through walls, but also to go through them mentally. Often friends came to her for help in finding lost articles. Mollie would seem to go into a kind of trance.

"I see your purse," she would say, "it has fallen behind the sofa." Or, "The bonds you are

51

looking for are hidden in the chimney in that unused wing of your house." Or, "The horse that ran away from your stable last night is at this moment cropping grass in Central Park, near 86th Street."

In every case, Mollie was right. And when her many friends did not visit her, she seemed to be able to mentally visit them. According to Judge Dailey, "She goes in spirit to her friends in different places, and sees what they are doing. She looks around the city, and sees what is happening. Then she comes back to herself in her room and reports where she has been and what she has seen."

Unbelievable? Perhaps. But many people actually observed evidence of Mollie's powers. According to Dr. W. R. Newbold of the University of Pennsylvania, they were all witnesses "whose truthfulness could not be questioned." So, if the stories about Mollie are true, there is one thing we must believe: She was not a woman to be pitied. In fact, for many reasons, she was a woman to be envied.

The Restless Statue

At the entrance to a military cemetery on the Saigon-Bienhoa highway in South Vietnam, there is a statue who walks and weeps — or so many Vietnamese say.

The statue is a war memorial, sculpted by the Vietnamese artist, Nguyen Thanh Tu. It is a heavy bronze figure of a seated soldier, thirteen feet high. The soldier's body is slumped wearily. Grief is in every line of his face. Across his knees lies his rifle, and a pack is strapped to his back.

Nguyen Thanh Tu named his creation *Sorrow*. There is something haunting about the bronze figure — in more ways than one.

In November 1966, the statue was put in place at the cemetery gate. Shortly afterward, excited South Vietnamese soldiers reported that they had met the statue walking on the highway. According to them, the figure had left its pedestal to warn them of an ambush ahead.

"We were moving along in a 20-vehicle convoy. The night was clear and moonlit. Suddenly a gigantic figure stepped out on the road ahead and held up a rifle, as if ordering us to stop. He said only three words: 'Go back! Ambush!' We did as he ordered — we were too stunned to do otherwise! He was dressed as we are, in battle dress, but it was plain to all of us that this was no human being. It was the statue!"

According to many of the Vietnamese peasants in the area, the statue cannot rest as long as there is fighting in Vietnam.

"He has seen too many die," said one woman. "It causes him so much pain that he must walk and grieve."

A Vietnamese military policeman agrees with the woman, and adds: "I have seen the statue step off his pedestal. It was in the morning when I was patrolling near the cemetery. It put its helmet and rifle down on the grass. Tears were rolling down its metal face. The sight was so terrible that I fell weeping on the ground myself. When I looked up again, the statue was back in place."

The villagers nearby believe that the statue wants to protect them. They say that on the eve of the 1968 Tet offensive, the great bronze figure walked from house to house and hammered with its fists on their doors to warn them that trouble was coming.

"Because of this, we were able to run away

and hide until the fighting was over. The statue saved our lives," insists one elderly man.

The village women often bring flowers, candles, rice, and bowls of water to the cemetery, and place them before the statue. When they are asked why, they say they have often heard the statue sigh and ask for food and water. They point out that when they return the next day, both food and water are gone.

Could animals or wanderers have drunk the water or eaten the food? "No, no," say the women. "No one would touch what is left for the statue. He knows it is for him alone."

When sculptor Nguyen Thanh Tu heard from the villagers that the statue often walks about the area at night, he examined its base carefully. "It looks secure, but there must be something to these stories. Perhaps I should go to a fortune-teller to find out the best way to put the statue in place so that it will stay there," he said.

But the people who live near the cemetery don't seem to worry about whether the statue roams or not. They know he is their friend.

The Kitten
That Would Not Die

Charles and Michelle Leret loved all their children, but perhaps had a special fondness for Rene, their youngest. Rene was only seven, but already his father was planning to send him to the university when he was old enough. "The boy is very intelligent and sensitive," Rene's teacher told Charles Leret. "He needs special attention."

Although Leret's earnings as a carpenter in a small French town were not great, he often showed his fondness for Rene by buying him special presents. One of these presents was a white kitten named Jacques. In no time at all, Jacques was Rene's most prized possession. It slept on his bed at night, and he took it to school with him during the day.

The summer of 1954 was hotter than usual,

and perhaps that is why Rene happened to sleep unusually late one Saturday morning. Jacques, however, was up early and wandered out of the house. The kitten reached the main road and started across — just as a truck barreled around the corner. The truck struck the kitten and killed it.

Horrified, the Lerets put off telling Rene what had happened that day and the next. They buried the tiny body and tried to decide how to break the news to their son. Finally, Michelle decided that the painful job must be done.

"Rene, I want to tell you about Jacques . . ." she began.

The boy smiled at her. "What is there to tell? He's right here, on my lap —" And the boy's hand stroked the air as if it were the silky fur of the kitten.

Michelle stared at her son. "Rene, what are you saying? Jacques is dead! He was run over by a truck!"

Rene jumped up, his face contorted. "No! Jacques is here with me! Can't you see him?" Bursting into tears, the boy ran out of the room.

He had spoken with such conviction that Michelle was almost frightened. Was Rene losing his mind? But her husband calmed her fears. "Rene has probably known all along that Jacques was killed. He is trying to comfort himself by pretending his pet is still here. He'll get over it if we are patient. In the meantime, we must humor him."

And humor him they did. They gave him food to put out for Jacques, and opened the door when Rene said that Jacques wanted to go out or come in.

Their patience lasted for weeks, but finally it came to an end. Charles Leret decided it was time for his son to face reality.

"You know that Jacques is gone for good," he told Rene. "And you must stop pretendng that he is still here with you!"

Rene looked at his father in bewilderment. "But Jacques is here. He's lying on the rug at your feet. Can't you see him?"

Nothing Charles Leret said or did could make Rene take back this amazing statement. Finally, he took the boy to Dr. Lefeve, a psychiatrist. The doctor made a number of mental and physical tests.

"There is nothing wrong with Rene," he told the astonished parents. "He is perfectly normal —"

"But what about his belief that Jacques is still alive?" demanded Michele Leret.

"It is a conviction," replied the doctor. "The boy is sane, but he believes the cat is still with him. For him it exists. He actually sees it. As far as Rene is concerned, nothing ever happened to take Jacques away from him."

"Does that mean, doctor, that our son is haunted by the ghost of a cat?" asked Charles Leret incredulously.

"I can't answer that question because I have no proof that such things as ghosts exist," replied the doctor. "However, there are some tests I can make."

Dr. Lefeve brought special instruments to the

Leret house. With one of them, he measured the temperature of each room before and after Rene entered it. He discovered that the temperature always dropped a few degrees when the boy came into a room.

"According to psychic investigators, a drop in the temperature means that a ghost is present," he explained to the puzzled Lerets.

Dr. Lefeve also dusted clean baseboards and doors in the house with a special powder. After a few moments, there appeared in the powder the marks of scratches like those made by a cat's claws.

Rene's mother and father did not know what to think. They could not bring themselves to believe in a cat ghost — but that was before the photograph came.

A week after Dr. Lefeve came to the house, the Lerets had Rene's photograph taken. He had posed, wearing his best suit, with his arms across his chest. Now the photograph had been delivered. The astonished adults could not believe their eyes! Looking at them from the picture was Jacques, curled up in Rene's arms.

Dr. Lefeve wrote out a statement. "I have examined the photograph and the negative carefully. There is no possibility that it was faked. Somehow the kitten was there when the picture was taken!"

The photograph of Rene with Jacques in his arms is now on file at the Paris headquarters of the French Society for Psychical Research. But how Jacques managed to be there to have his picture taken is still an unsolved mystery.

The Drawing
That Warned of Death

On an autumn afternoon in Baltimore, Maryland, Mrs. Emily Tobin sat talking on the telephone. As she talked, she doodled on a scratch pad.

When the conversation was over, she tore off the top of the scratch pad and was about to throw it away. But her hand stopped in midair as she gazed unbelievingly at what she had drawn.

The picture that met her eyes was indeed an alarming one. It showed the front of a house, with heavy vines framing the door. A flight of wrought iron steps led down into a garden from the door. At the foot of the steps, Mrs. Tobin had drawn a picture of herself lying face down in a puddle of water.

"My hand shook as I held the drawing," Mrs. Tobin remembers. "I could scarcely believe my eyes. It was not only the subject that shocked me, but the fact that it was such a good drawing. Now, everyone who knows me knows that I can't draw at all — even though my father was a well-known commercial artist. Yet, absentmindedly, I had managed to create a gruesome work of art!

"I felt like burning the thing, but something made me put it aside until my husband came home. I had a hard time making him believe that I had really drawn it. 'You must have hidden talent,' he said. 'But why did you draw such a morbid picture?'"

Eventually Mrs. Tobin put the drawing away in her desk and forgot about it. Months passed. Then in the late spring, she received a telegram telling her that an elderly aunt had died in a small town in Virginia.

"There were no other relatives to straighten out her affairs, so I packed a suitcase and took the train to my aunt's hometown. She had been living in a house on the outskirts of town. When I first saw the house, I had that funny feeling they call déjà vu, as if I'd been there before, even though I knew I hadn't."

Mrs. Tobin soon forgot this feeling as she busied herself with the job of disposing of her aunt's property. It was almost three weeks before all the work was done. On the morning of her last day in the house, she was awakened by the sound of rain lashing against the windows.

"The rain poured down all morning. I waited

61

as long as I could, but I had a train to catch so finally I picked up my suitcase and went out into the downpour. I noticed that the garden was pretty well flooded with about three or four inches of water. But as I started down the front steps, my ankle turned and I tumbled all the way to the concrete at the bottom. I must have struck my head, for I blacked out."

When Mrs. Tobin came to, she thought she was dreaming. She was leaning back in the seat of a car, and her husband was bending over her.

"Thank heavens," he said. "I thought at first you were dead."

"What happened?" Mrs. Tobin managed to gasp. "How did you get here?" She was now aware that her clothing was soaking wet, and her head was throbbing. But she forgot her discomfort as she listened to her husband's explanation.

"I think we owe the fact that you're still alive to your father. Yes, I know he's been dead for years — but I dreamed about him last night. He was shaking that crazy drawing you made in my face, and he kept saying over and over, 'Hurry . . . danger . . .' I woke up about dawn in a cold sweat, knowing I had to get to you right away — but not knowing why. I just jumped in the car and broke all speed records getting here. Thank God I did. You were unconscious, lying face down in the water at the foot of those steps! If I'd been a minute later, you might have drowned!"

Emily Tobin closed her eyes. Realization flooded her mind. "Of course," she murmured.

"I really didn't draw that picture. Somehow, Dad reached out and guided my hand. He was trying to warn me about this house . . . that's why the place seemed so familiar to me when I came. But I didn't know what he was trying to tell me, so he had to contact you in the dream!"

Mrs. Tobin still shivers when she remembers what almost happened to her. "Suppose my husband had just turned over and gone back to sleep! I've framed the drawing to remind myself how lucky I am. When people ask me the name of the artist, I say very proudly, 'My father.'"

The Strange Case
of the Upside-Down Tenants

"I am afraid to go into my apartment," the elderly Frenchwoman told the magistrate.

The woman's name was Madame Blerotti, and what she had to say made no sense at all. Outside the magistrate's office, Paris basked in the spring sunshine of 1917. But inside, Madame Blerotti shivered as though she sat in a tomb.

"I am afraid to go home," she repeated.

The apartment Madame Blerotti complained about was located in the Rue Montreuil. She lived there on the top floor of a house with her son and brother-in-law. Until lately, the place had seemed pleasant and comfortable enough. But a few weeks ago, a peculiar thing had begun to happen.

"Each time I step through my front door, I find myself upside down, walking on my hands!" explained Madame Blerotti.

The magistrate stared at the old woman. What was she talking about? She was certainly too old to be perambulating about, walking on her hands! Was she mentally deranged. Perhaps he had better humor her.

"You remain here," he told her. "I will send a policeman to your apartment to investigate."

A young policeman was ordered to go to the Rue Montreuil. He climbed the three flights to the Blerotti apartment, and knocked on the door. As he stood waiting for someone to answer, he began to feel uneasy. "There was a strange atmosphere about the top floor," he reported later. "I am not a fanciful man, but I felt I was being watched by someone of a malicious nature — a prankster waiting to see me make a fool of myself!"

He was almost relieved to see the apartment door open. Madame Blerotti's son Andre stood there. When he heard what the policeman had to say, he nodded. "It is perfectly true what my mother says. I cannot explain it, but whenever any of us cross this threshold, we are *forced* to walk on our hands for a few minutes."

"Forced?" demanded the policeman. "By whom?"

Andre shrugged. "No one — or perhaps I should say no one we can see. But we have no choice. It is as though we were grabbed and our feet pulled straight into the air."

"You had better come with me and tell this

story to the magistrate," replied the policeman.

"Very well," said Andre, "but I suggest we stop at the cafe on the corner where my uncle works. He will also come with me and back up my story."

Within a short time the entire Blerotti family had assembled to face the magistrate. But their testimony only seemed to confuse the situation.

"The policeman tells me you were standing on your feet when you answered the door. Yet the three of you tell me you cannot help walking on your hands. What is this nonsense?" shouted the magistrate.

"It is the truth," replied Andre. "We are only compelled to walk on our hands when we enter the apartment. The feeling lasts but a short time. However, when it hits you, you cannot resist it."

Madame Blerotti's brother, a stout middle-aged man, chimed in. "Do I look like an athlete who likes to do calisthenics?" he asked. "I could not do a handstand by myself if I tried, yet each time I enter the apartment, there I am — feet in the air, padding about on both hands. The situation is intolerable. Something must be done. You are paid to protect citizens. Protect us, then!"

This was too much for the magistrate. Leaving the Blerottis in custody of the young policeman, he stormed off to the Rue Montreuil. "Are your tenants insane?" he asked the manager of the house. "They seem to think something is forcing them to do acrobatics."

The manager shrugged. "You must judge for

yourself." He led the way upstairs to the Blerotti apartment. Unlocking the door, he stepped back so that the magistrate could enter.

The magistrate never forgot what happened next. "An invisible wind seemed to push me forward. It forced me on all fours. Then my feet were slowly lifted into the air so that I stood on my hands. I had the distinct sensation that someone hovered near, laughing at me. Suddenly my feet were released, and I fell to the floor."

Back in his office, the magistrate faced the Blerottis. "I can do nothing for you," he informed them. "What troubles you is not a police matter. In my opinion, your apartment is infected by an evil force. I would suggest you ask your parish priest for help in disinfecting it."

A report on the Blerottis' troubled apartment appeared in the May 1, 1907, *London Daily Mail*, an English newspaper. But there were no follow-up reports to tell us what, if anything, the Blerottis did to disinfect their home. We can only wonder whether an unseen something still haunts the top floor of a house on the Rue Montreuil, waiting to turn life upside down for anyone who lives there.

The Frightened Ghost

      Visiting in-laws may not always be a happy experience, but it is seldom a terrifying one. When Henry and Eileen Sweeney set off to spend a few days with Eileen's parents in Mamaroneck, New York, they didn't expect to have an experience that would send shivers down their spines for years to come.

Mrs. Sweeney's parents lived in a big, old-fashioned house, and the young couple were given a bedroom on the third floor. On the first morning, Henry Sweeney got up late. He decided to go down to the kitchen to make himself some breakfast, since he was sure everyone else in the household had already eaten.

As Henry started downstairs, he saw a strange woman coming up the stairs toward him. Was she a neighbor? he wondered. If so, it struck him as odd that she should be wearing a long white robe. He also noticed that she was tall and slender, and had either light blonde or gray hair.

"When she was about fifteen feet away from me, she stopped abruptly and looked right into my eyes. She seemed startled. She brushed past me hurriedly, turned to the right, and disappeared into one of the bedrooms on the third floor. As she went into the room, she glanced back over her shoulder with a look of fear."

Puzzled, Henry went on downstairs. His mother-in-law was in the kitchen, and he asked her what the strange woman was doing on the third floor.

"To my surprise, Mom turned pale and burst into tears. She said, 'I thought I was losing my mind. I've seen her too — but no one else has. I don't know who or *what* she is!' "

Alarmed, Henry ran back up to the third floor. He searched all the rooms, beginning with the one he had seen the strange woman disappear into. As he half-expected, there was no one there.

For the rest of the day, he could not get the woman out of his mind. That evening, he decided to tell the rest of the family about his experience. His mother-in-law, who had said nothing before for fear of being laughed at, backed him up. The others looked thoughtful. Then his sister-in-law spoke up.

"You know I've never liked to go up to the third floor, and that I won't sleep there. Well, I'll tell you all why now. I've heard noises I can't account for when I'm up there alone —

footsteps, someone humming in the bathroom. I couldn't explain it, so I didn't mention it until now."

Perhaps, suggested one of Eileen's uncles, the woman was deranged and had slipped into the house often. He pointed out that the family seldom locked their doors.

The explanation was comforting — until the next night. Henry and his wife had retired early, but he found himself unable to sleep. He was about to turn on the light and read when he saw the same white-robed woman walk quickly past his side of the bed. She did not look at him, but went into the closet on the other side of the room.

"I turned on the light, jumped out of bed, and checked the closet. There was no one there. She couldn't have gotten out of the room, for the door was still closed as it had been when I first saw her pass the bed. My wife had awakened by this time, and she suggested we check the rest of the house. We found no one there who shouldn't have been."

The next morning, Henry again woke late. His wife and her sister had left early on a shopping expedition. But someone was splashing about in the bathroom. He waited for a while, but the noises of bathing went on. Finally he went downstairs, only to find the rest of the family at breakfast.

"That's strange," he said. "I thought one of you was taking a bath." The family looked at each other in surprise as Henry ran back upstairs to look in the bathroom. No one was there.

The next morning there were no unexplained sounds on the third floor, but surprises were still in store for Henry. As he entered the kitchen, he saw his mother-in-law through the open door. She was in the backyard hanging up wash. Standing just behind her was the woman in the white robe.

"Now I was sure she was a neighbor," Henry recalls. "I called out 'Good morning,' to her and got a nod in return. My mother-in-law, however, paid no attention to her. The woman remained standing where she was when my mother-in-law came back into the kitchen.

"Aren't you on speaking terms with your neighbor?" Henry asked.

"What neighbor?" his mother-in-law asked.

"The one who was standing near you while you hung up the wash. She's still there, watching us. Turn around and you'll see her."

His mother-in-law began to tremble. "No, no! I won't look. I don't want to see her!" she wailed.

Suddenly Henry lost patience. He ran into the backyard toward the woman. She moved quickly away, still facing him. In a minute she had disappeared into the yard next door.

Hoping to head her off, Henry ran into the alley. About fifty feet away he saw the woman standing and watching him. Her eyes were full of fear. As he ran toward her, she moved swiftly backward, always keeping a distance of about fifty feet between them.

Finally Henry tired of the chase. He gave up and returned to the house. No doubt, he thought, the woman would return there also in time.

Henry was right. A few nights later he and Eileen's uncle sat watching television on the first floor. Gradually he became aware that someone else was in the room. He turned and saw the woman standing there.

"I had made my up mind that she wouldn't get away from me again. I literally flew from my chair. She whirled and ran out into the front hallway to the stairway."

Up to the third floor landing, Henry pursued the woman in white. He was so close that he felt he could make a grab for her robe and bring her to a halt. He reached out.

"I got the shock of my life! The woman had vanished. Before me floated a length of gray, spidery, gauzy stuff that looked like chiffon. Then, slowly, it too seemed to fade away."

Henry and his wife had had enough of the house. They ended their visit and went home. Eileen's family also decided to move out of the house. They made up their minds to do so when Eileen's sister met an invisible something on the stairway. It shoved her aside and rushed by.

Was it the lady with the frightened eyes? Had she decided to become invisible so that the living could no longer chase her through the house?

Girl with a Problem

Jennie Bramwell was an orphan. Until the age of 14, her only home had been the Belleville Orphanage in Ontario. Then Jennie got lucky. She was adopted by a Mrs. Robert Dawson.

Jennie seemed fairly happy in her new home, although there were certain problems of adjustment. Mrs. Dawson expected the girl to do a certain amount of chores around the cottage, and Jennie seemed to resent this. But things went along smoothly enough until Jennie was stricken with meningitis.

The doctor who was called in on the case walked into a kind of waking nightmare. At his first attempt to take Jennie's temperature, the thermometer flew out of his hand and embedded itself with penetrating force in the wall over the bed. Then the door to the bedroom began to bang shut over and over until Mrs. Dawson pushed a heavy chair against it. And the bed upon which Jennie lay *walked* — at least that's the word the doctor later used — into the middle of the room.

By the time the doctor got back to his own office, he managed to convince himself that all the confusion had some kind of natural explanation. But not for long. About three o'clock in the morning, he received a frantic message from Mrs. Dawson: "Jennie's burning up!"

He rushed to the Dawson house, and found that the message was no mere figure of speech. True, Jennie's temperature had climbed alarmingly — but the bed and the pillows upon which she lay were charred along their outside edges.

"How did this happen?" the doctor demanded.

Mrs. Dawson shook her head, and began to cry. "I don't know! I had gone to get some cold compresses to bathe her forehead, when I smelled smoke. I ran back here and saw little flames along the edge of the mattress and the pillows. Jennie was lying there unconscious. I grabbed a blanket and smothered the flames. For heavens' sake, doctor, what's going on?"

The doctor had no time for conjecture. Jennie's illness had reached the crisis point, and he had his hands full trying to save her life. Later, he did wonder whether Mrs. Dawson's carelessness had somehow started the fire, and whether she had been too shocked and ashamed to admit it. But at the time, the important thing was to save Jennie and start her back on the road to recovery.

The convalescence was a slow one, and Jennie often seemed to have spells of drowsiness that put her into a trancelike state. Mrs. Dawson soon learned to dread these spells. More than once they were the forerunners of serious trouble.

In one such state, Jennie suddenly screamed and pointed to the ceiling over her bed. Fire had broken out there in a circular patch. Mrs. Dawson grabbed a bucket of water and put out the flames, thoroughly soaking Jennie in the process.

Perhaps allowing Jennie to move about the house would cut down on her drowsiness, Mrs. Dawson thought, and speed her recovery. The next day she handed Jennie her slippers and robe, and told her she might get up. Listlessly the girl obeyed, but then sank into a chair by her bedroom window. Suddenly she stood up and leaned out of the window.

"There's a fire in the kitchen downstairs!" she cried.

No sooner had this fire been put out by Mrs. Dawson and a neighbor, then smoke and flames appeared at the base of a parlor wall. More neighbors rushed to help — and found themselves working overtime. As soon as one blaze was extinguished, another broke out elsewhere in the Dawson cottage. At one point, a picture on a wall burst into flames.

During the following week almost one hundred small fires occurred in the Dawson home. Furniture, wallpaper, curtains, towels, and rugs were singed or consumed by flames. There was no fire department in the area in which Mrs. Dawson lived, so she had to rely on her neighbors for help. As she struggled to keep her home from burning down around her, an uncomfortable suspicion was forming in her mind. Jennie!—Jennie had something to do with those terrible fires.

"I was sure the girl didn't actually set fire to things herself," Mrs. Dawson admitted. "She was seldom in the same room where a fire would break out. But she would know where the fires were before anyone else did, and she'd point them out to us."

On one day fifty small fires broke out in the house. The family cat, sitting on Mrs. Dawson's lap, suddenly caught fire and rushed out of the house. There the flames died out, but the animal was badly burned and had to be destroyed.

Because she now felt uneasy in Jennie's presence, Mrs. Dawson sent her back to school the following week. "She didn't want to go because she said she didn't feel strong enough, but I couldn't stand it any longer. I thought we might all have some peace if she had studies to occupy her mind."

The state of peace lasted for just one week. There were no more fires in the Dawson house, and Mrs. Dawson began to consider having repairs made. But her new found sense of security vanished when Jennie's teacher asked her to come to school on the following Monday afternoon.

The classroom was a shambles. The blackboard was cracked and splintered. The door of the room hung by one hinge. And the center of the ceiling was blackened and charred by fire.

"What happened?" gasped Mrs. Dawson.

The teacher was white and tight-lipped. "I must ask you not to send Jennie back to this school again," she said in a trembling voice. "Her presence is disruptive. Since she returned to school — well, you can see for yourself that we had a fire in the ceiling. The desk under that charred spot happens to be Jennie's. And several times fires have broken out in my desk."

"But the door . . . the blackboard . . ." whispered Mrs. Dawson.

"That happened when I told Jennie she would have to work extra time to make up lessons she missed while she was ill. She turned beet red and just glared at me. Then there was a terrific cracking noise — the blackboard! The hinge flew off the door at the same time and struck me in the shoulder."

"But how could Jennie possibly cause such things to happen?" said Mrs. Dawson desperately.

"I don't know, Mrs. Dawson. But wherever she is, there seems to be trouble. The fires in your house — I know no one ever saw her set them, but terrible things seem to happen around the girl. For the safety of my students, I can't have Jennie in this school."

Mrs. Dawson left the school with the word *safety* ringing in her mind. She was convinced now that Jennie was somehow dangerous. The next morning she packed the girl's clothes, and drove her back to the orphanage. After that, there were no more fires in the Dawson home.

Was Jennie a victim of mass hysteria? Was it only coincidence that fires broke out when she was near? These are possible answers to a puzzling question, but psychic investigators have come up with another one. According to them, Jennie Bramwell was the agent of a *poltergeist.*

Poltergeist is an old German word meaning a noisy or mischievous ghost. But parapsychologists say that a poltergeist is not a ghost at all, but a projection of the subconscious mind of a living human being. In the opinion of these experts, these subconscious projections take the form of energy. Dishes and furniture may fly through the air. Objects may be hurled against walls and windows. Fires may break out.

Poltergeist activity often seems to have its source in young people of adolescent age. According to the London Council for Psychical Investigation, nine out of ten of such cases seem to be young girls like Jennie Bramwell. Often such young people are emotionally disturbed, and their anxieties and aggressive instincts seem to flare out in poltergeist outbreaks.

A young person who seems to be the agent for poltergeist disturbances is like the center of a storm. He or she may not move a muscle while energy generated by emotion does the damage. Parapsychologists point out that electricity is a physical energy which can be converted into heat, light, and motion. Is it possible that the emotional energy of some disturbed persons might work the same way?

Monsters on the Loose

Perhaps you think that monsters are only found in science fiction and horror movies. Many people all over the world would disagree with you. Mr. J. F. Phillips of Wellington, New Zealand, is one of them: He met a monster.

It happened when Mr. Phillips was fishing on the Marokopa River in 1961. Since he hadn't had a bite on his line for hours, he was unprepared for the tremendous pull he suddenly felt. He pulled back, and after much effort, finally dragged his catch up on the riverbank.

"It was an enormous eel, with a head as big as a sheep's. It had very sharp teeth, and it bit right through the line. Then it started after me!" As he fled, Mr. Phillips said he could hear the creature's teeth *grinding*. "I climbed up the nearest tree. For a while it thrashed around on the bank, and then slid back into the water. Only then did I feel it was safe to come down."

If you appreciate Mr. Phillips' monster, how about the one that is said to dwell in Hollow Block Lake near Portland, Indiana? Those who claim to have seen this thing say that it is as big as an automobile, and square in shape. It likes to rise up out of the water and scare people who happen to be fishing on the lake. If the sight of it fails to frighten fishermen, the Hollow Block Lake monster has a hideous scream guaranteed to make your hair stand on end.

So far, the monster of Hollow Block Lake has never hurt anyone. But there are monsters who seem bent on destruction. Ogopogo is this kind of a monster.

Ogopogo's hunting ground is Lake Okanagan, in southwest British Columbia. On the rocks near the lake, Indians who lived there before the white men came painted a picture of Ogopogo. The painting shows a creature with a thick body like a gigantic python, and the head of a horse.

According to the legends of these Indians, Ogopogo (their name for him was Naitaka) lived at the bottom of the lake. When he was hungry, he would rise to the surface to claim a victim — usually someone trying to cross the lake in a canoe. With one lash of his huge, powerful tail, Ogopogo would overturn the canoe. Then the great, fang-lined jaws would drag the struggling victim beneath the waters.

There was no chance of swimming to shore and safety if Ogopogo marked you for his own, say the Indians. The monster could swim twenty miles an hour, faster than man.

Early white settlers in this part of British Columbia heard the legend, and christened the creature Ogopogo. The thought of a giant thing dwelling in the lake didn't frighten them away, it did make them cautious. Farmers who liked to swim their horses across the lake to pastures on the other side were careful first to throw a dead sheep or pig into the waters to keep Ogopogo busy.

A farmer named John McDougal often took his horses across this way. He would tie them to lines attached to the back of his canoe, and let them swim as he paddled. But one day he set out, only to realize halfway across that he had forgotten to bring Ogopogo a pig.

Should he paddle back and get one? No, he decided, the horses would be too tired to make the swim over again. He crossed his fingers and went on, paddling a little faster now.

Suddenly one horse began to thrash about. Then it vanished below the water as if the lake had gulped it down. McDougal put down his paddle and grabbed the rope that tied the other horse to the canoe. He pulled it taut, hoping to keep the animal above water. But it, too, was being dragged under.

Frantically, McDougal hung onto the rope. But the weight of the drowning horse was tipping the canoe's stern into the water. At any moment he would be thrown into the lake, at the mercy of whatever had seized his horses.

In desperation McDougal got out his knife and cut the rope. Then he paddled as hard as he could for the nearest shore. He didn't bother even to look over his shoulder for the horses. The Indians had told him that Ogopogo never gives up what it takes.

In July 1959, newspaper publisher Dick Miller and several friends were taking a vacation cruise on Lake Okanagan. Miller's attention was attracted by a sudden wash of foam that disturbed the surface of the middle of the lake, as if somethng were moving swiftly beneath it.

Suddenly, an immense dark-green shape, with a head "something like an oversize horse's," rose out of the foamy water about 200 feet away. Miller yelled, and grabbed his field glasses. At his shout his friends rushed to the side of the boat to look at the thing.

In a later report Miller wrote that he and his friends estimated that the creature's head was about eight feet long and seven feet wide. "The length of the thing was anywhere from sixty to ninety feet long. As it swam, its body bunched into five humps which seemed the size of small hillocks."

Miller ordered the boat to steer nearer the creature, but Ogopogo evidently didn't care to be examined at close quarters. First the head sank beneath the waters, then the great body.

If there really is an Ogopogo, what could it be? Professor James Miloed, zoologist of the University of Manitoba, has a theory. "Great

82

reptiles lived in the prehistoric inland sea that once occupied this area. Their descendants may have survived into modern times, and still inhabit the lake. I'll admit I'm skeptical about this, but it is a scientific possibility."

Is Ogopogo a kind of living dinosaur? Is he related to Nessie, the monster that's supposed to dwell in Scotland's Loch Ness? Both Nessie and Ogopogo seem to fit the same description — horselike head, huge snakey barrellike body, dark-green color.

Scientists are investigating both Loch Ness and Lake Okanagan. They think it is possible that Ogopogo and Nessie may not be dinosaurs, but some kind of giant eel. In certain parts of Loch Ness the water is about 800 feet deep. Okanagan is almost twice as deep. Such vast depths could shelter creatures of great size. But before zoologists will admit that there really are monsters in these lakes, they want a full-size specimen to study.

If the zoologists would pay a visit to New Hamburg, Ontario, they might be able to trap their specimen on dry land — according to Police Chief George Thomas.

Reports Chief Thomas, "a slimy, three-toed monster" strolls around New Hamburg's streets at night. The Chief once took a shot at it but missed. It presented a fair-size target, standing about 10 feet high. It was greenish-brown in color, had a powerful tail covered with scales, and four legs with three toes apiece.

"My patience is running out," says Chief Thomas. "If it shows up again, I'll shoot it on sight."

Other citizens of New Hamburg back the Chief up, and say that they too have seen the monster. Some of them claim that it has been promenading through their town for about three years. "But they don't like to talk about it," Chief Thomas says. "They're respectable, quiet folk who wouldn't want other people to accuse them of drinking."

Dreamers Who Saw Death

Mary Daughtery was fond of saying that when she went to sleep, she didn't waste time dreaming. As for nightmares, she never had them!

However, on the night of November 7, 1965, Mary had a zinger of a nightmare — one that neither she nor her husband George will ever forget.

"I was standing on a hill in the night. Lightning flashed and thunder rolled overhead. Then a very bright light appeared in the sky and seemed to rush toward the earth. There was a shattering impact, and smoke and screams filled the air."

Through the smoke Mary glimpsed a hand lying on the ground. It filled her with a sense of dread, but she moved closer until she could see first the arm, then the shattered body to which the hand belonged. "Somebody, please help!" she screamed, and men appeared with a large wicker basket. They put the body into the basket and went away.

Mary was still screaming when she awoke. Her husband was bending over her, shaking her.

"What on earth is the matter?" he asked.

"I just saw you killed in a plane crash! I saw your body carried away! Oh, please, George, cancel your flight to Cincinnati."

"Nonsense," her husband replied. "I've made dozens of flights, and nothing ever happens. You just had a nightmare, but if it will make you feel any better — I'll call you the minute I get to Cincinnati."

In vain Mary begged him to put off his trip. George only laughed and joked about people who thought they had premonitions. But as he drove to the airport a strange feeling began to weigh upon him. A plane, flying low overhead, made his heart thud with something like fear. At last he pulled up beside a telephone booth, and called American Airlines, cancelling his space on Flight 383. Instead, he drove to the railway station and took the train for Cincinnati.

That evening, Flight 383 ran into a heavy thunderstorm while trying to land at the Greater Cincinnati Airport. The plane crashed into a hill. Mary shuddered as she saw scenes of the wreckage on the television news. She closed her eyes as rescue workers began to carry bodies away in wicker baskets.

Thanks to her dream, her husband was not one of the dead or injured.

Not every dreamer gets the kind of cooperation that George Daughtery gave his wife. In 1950, John Bradley had a dream of impending danger. But when he tried to warn others, they laughed at him.

Bradley was a teacher in the small English town of Houghton. He was also an enthusiastic amateur naturalist. His class enjoyed his hobby almost as much as he did, because he often took them on field trips through the countryside.

The dream came one week before a planned field trip. Bradley saw himself leading the class along a country lane near a churchyard. He realized that if he led them through the churchyard and along the river, they would be taking a timesaving shortcut.

In his dream Bradley ordered two of the older boys to lead the way, while he walked at the end of the line to keep the smaller children from straggling.

As they passed through the churchyard, Bradley felt the ground tremble. A hideous cracking sound ripped the silence. Then something huge and dark rushed toward him as an immense elm tree crashed down on the line of children.

As clearly as though he was still awake, John could hear the shrieks of the children. He could see their arms and legs sticking out from under the tree.

On the way to school he thought a great deal

87

about the dream. Never had he had one so vivid. By the time he reached the classroom, he had decided to cancel the field trip. But he felt he owed the children an explanation.

"Do any of you believe in dreams?" he asked. "Do you think dreams can warn of possible danger? I had a dream like that last night."

But when he told the class about his dream, many of the pupils snickered and laughed. Some of the other teachers were even more scornful. One suggested that Bradley's dream was really a subconscious expression of his dislike for his class.

Bradley also had to undergo some good-natured joking from some of the parents of his students. "Had any good dreams lately?" was one standard greeting for days. Maybe he was behaving like a fool, Bradley decided. He announced to the class that the postponed field trip would take place after all.

"Only this time," he told them, "there will be no shortcuts. In deference to my dream, we will take the long way around."

The children agreed and followed Bradley's orders during the hike without protest. Some of them smiled a little when the churchyard came in view, but they all marched obediently the long way around to the river.

The older boys who were leading the group called a halt at a wooden bridge.

"Which way, sir? Shall we cross here, or go on until we come to the footpath?"

Bradley hesitated. Footpath — there was something about the idea that made him uneasy.

"Take the bridge," he ordered.

Chattering, the children began to file across the bridge. Then, as in his dream, Bradley heard the terrible cracking sound. Beyond, where the footpath began, an immense elm tottered on its base, then crashed to the ground.

In the silence that followed, the children stared at each other, then at their teacher. If they had taken the shortcut, they would have reached the footpath a few minutes before. If they had been on the footpath, many of them might now be dead!

After that, no one in Houghton made jokes about John Bradley's dream. In fact, it became not uncommon for the parents of his students to drop by now and then to consult him.

"I had this peculiar dream last night," was often the standard opening on these visits. "I'll tell you about it, and then you can tell me what you think it means."

Cats That Came Back

Do animals have ESP? Do some of them establish mental bonds with their owners that neither time nor space can break? The case of the cat called Li-Ping offers one answer.

Li-Ping was the pet of Vivian Allgood of Canton, Ohio. In April 1955, Vivian decided to take a job in Orlando, Florida. It wasn't altogether a happy decision, because it meant she would have to leave Li-Ping behind with her sister.

A month later Vivian was settled in Florida. She wrote her sister, asking that Li-Ping be sent down to her because she felt she could not be parted from her pet any longer. Having mailed the letter she went to visit a friend.

As she walked up the steps to the friend's

porch, something moving on the street caught her eye. A bedraggled, starved-looking cat was coming toward her — a cat that reminded her of Li-Ping!

"But that's absurd," she murmured. "How could it be Li-Ping?" Her cat was at least 1,500 miles away.

As if it heard what she said, the cat stopped and stared at her. Then it ran straight to her. She picked it up and looked at it unbelievingly. It was scrawny, its fur was missing in patches, its feet were torn and raw — but it was without a doubt Li-Ping!

Perhaps the cat saw doubt in her face. It opened its mouth, and a faint squeak came out. That settled the question of its identity for Valerie. Li-Ping's vocal chords had been damaged when he was a kitten. The only sound he had ever been able to produce was a faint squeak.

A call to Vivian's sister verified the fact that Li-Ping had been missing for weeks. "He ran away after you left town," her sister said. "I've been trying to get up nerve enough to tell you ever since."

There are several questions that still puzzle Valerie. How did Li-Ping manage to travel over a thousand miles on foot to reach her? How did he know where to find her? She was not even at her own house at the time, but at the house of a friend!

At the Institute of Parapsychology at Duke University, cats are regularly tested for ESP. Many cases of cats who, like Li-Ping, managed to track down their owners — even when the owners had moved across the continent — have been checked out here.

"To know how a cat's mind works, I would have to be a cat," says Dr. Helmut Schmidt of the Institute. "Our tests show that cats do exhibit ESP, and that's all we really know for sure."

Another cat who refused to be separated from his owner was Felix of the town of St. Kilda, Australia. Felix belonged to an elderly man, and when the man died, the cat seemed to fall into an almost human state of deep depression. Mrs. King, the old man's daughter, decided to take Felix to her home in the city of Melbourne. But there his condition became worse. He refused both food and comfort, and spent his days lying in front of a picture of the old man in Mrs. King's bedroom.

Mrs. King grew seriously worried about the cat. "He's grieving just like a human being. Maybe a change of scene would cheer him up. Let's take him on a picnic out in the countryside."

The Kings packed up a picnic lunch and drove off with Felix in the car. But when they stopped at a pleasant spot in the country for lunch, the cat jumped out and ran off. The Kings waited in vain for him to return. But when it began to grow dark, they returned home, hoping he might have gone back there. Felix failed to show up.

Ten days went by, and Mrs. King resigned

herself to the fact that she would probably never see Felix again. Since it was a Sunday, she and her husband decided to visit her father's grave in the Melbourne Cemetery.

At the cemetery the Kings got a surprise. There was Felix, pacing back and forth like a guard at Mrs. King's father's grave!

The cemetery was more than ten miles from the King house. Felix had never been there in his life. Yet the invisible tie which bound the cat to the old man had somehow led the cat to the grave. Knowing Felix would never leave the grave, Mrs. King gave in and paid a cemetery attendant to feed him.

No cat ever traveled further than Sabot, a dark gray tiger cat with seven toes on each foot. Sabot belonged to Mrs. Sylvia Burke of Chicago, Illinois. When the cat died of enteritis in 1968, Mrs. Burke felt she had suffered a great loss.

"I have no children, so Sabot was an especially close friend to me," Mrs. Burke remembers. "She was an intelligent animal who liked to invent little games. One of her favorite games was to hide, then jump out and land on my shoulder if I failed to find her quickly."

Two years after Sabot's death, Mrs. Burke was planting bulbs in her garden. Suddenly, almost out of nowhere, a cat leaped on her shoulder — a white cat she had never seen before.

"At least I thought I had never seen it before — at first," says Mrs. Burke. "But when I lifted it off my shoulder, I saw that it had seven toes on each foot, like Sabot! And when I looked into that cat's eyes, I was sure I was looking again at Sabot — somehow come back to me in another body."

There are, of course, many cats who have seven toes. And many cats are fond of leaping up on a convenient human shoulder. Was Mrs. Burke reading too much into these coincidences? She doesn't think so. For her the clincher came when she let the white cat into her house.

"After Sabot died, I packed her toys in a box and put them away on a closet shelf. The white cat went at once to that closet and leaped up on the shelf. She dragged the box out and pushed it off so that it fell on the floor. Then she fished out the toys and began to play with them. If she didn't have Sabot's memories, how can you explain that?"

Lights from Nowhere

        If there are such things as visitors from outer space, what might they look like? Would they be human in appearance, or insectlike, or would they resemble plants? Or could it be possible, as Mrs. Ellin of Mobile, Alabama, suggests, that such a visitor might simply be a glowing light?

Ellin is not the real name of the woman to whom the following strange thing happened. She has requested that her real name be kept secret. "Like most people, I don't enjoy being held up to scorn and ridicule," she says. "But I saw what I saw, and so did my husband."

On a morning in June 1960, Mrs. Ellin was sitting with her husband in the dining room. "From where I sat, I could see into the kitchen and most of the living room," she remembers.

Suddenly, a brilliant rose-colored flash lit up

the kitchen. "What was that?" exclaimed Mr. Ellin.

His wife didn't answer. She was staring in astonishment at the wall fan in the kitchen. A glowing, rose-colored *something* seemed to be crawling between the blades of the fan. It was vaguely circular in outline, and it appeared to move by bunching itself up and then stretching out.

"Once it struggled through the fan, it rose to the ceiling. It clung for a brief second to the light fixture," recalls Mrs. Ellin. "Then, almost too fast for the eye to follow, it rushed into the dining room. It made for a corner where the wall joins the ceiling, almost as though it was trying to find a crack to escape through. It was about two and a half feet across at the thickest part."

The glowing thing seemed to inch along the top of the wall for a few more minutes as if seeking an escape route. Then it suddenly glowed a dark rose pink —and vanished!

"We never saw it again," says Mrs. Ellin, "but I'm certain it was alive and intelligent. It behaved like an animal that finds itself locked in a strange place. But how it got there or where it came from — that's the mystery. Was our house a place in which it took refuge, or was it like a crevice you might fall into while exploring an unknown wilderness?"

A mysterious lifesaving light appeared to R. B. Davis of Cedar Key, Florida, in 1954. Davis and two other men were on the water, heading home from a campsite. But as night fell the winds rose, growing steadily in strength.

Pushed by the wind, the waves increased in height. The boat began to take on water and the outboard motor sputtered and died. To keep the boat afloat Davis tore the motor loose and threw it over the side. Then the wind took over, tossing the boat wildly about.

The men could do nothing but cling to the sides of the boat and pray. Their position was perilous. At any moment the mountainous waves might capsize the boat, throwing them all into the water. There was also the danger that they might be run down by a larger craft in the pitch blackness.

Suddenly a light appeared a few feet away. It was a deep red in color and it seemed to skim the tops of the waves ahead of them. It moved back and forth, as if beckoning them.

The men watched for a few minutes in fascination, as the light gyrated. At times it seemed to hover. Then it would dart toward them, then away. Its red glow pulsated steadily.

"As I watched it I began to wonder if it wasn't offering to guide us. I said as much to my companions. I may be crazy, but as if it had heard me, the light stopped moving. It hung there before us, utterly still, while we ripped loose the seat boards to use as paddles."

When the men started paddling with the boards, the light resumed its motion ahead of them. Hardly daring to hope, they followed it, paddling even when exhaustion numbed them. Shortly before dawn the wind stopped and the light seemed to become fainter. Its motion stopped again and it hung as if watching them.

As the sky lightened, the three men saw why the light was no longer moving. Land lay ahead, a stretch of the Florida beach. With their last ounce of strength, Davis and his friends made it to shore. When they looked up again, the light was gone.

Later Davis sent out inquiries about the source of the light. No one offered any explanations. Obviously it could not have been on a plane, a ship, or a helicopter.

"We don't know where it came from, or why," Davis admits. "All we do know is that if it hadn't acted as our guide, we would probably all be dead now."

The Girl in the Snow

It began to snow early on that December day in 1880. By evening the streets of Philadelphia were blocked with drifts, and the wind howled and raged.

In his warm and comfortable bedroom, Dr. S. Weir Mitchell settled down to a well-earned sleep. As he drifted off, the click of snow hurled against his window faded into a kind of staccato lullaby.

Then another sound took over, jerking Dr. Mitchell out of unconsciousness. The doorbell downstairs was ringing violently.

Reluctantly, Mitchell pulled on his robe and stumbled downstairs. Who was brave enough to come to his house through the storm — brave enough or desperate enough?

As he opened the front door, he could scarcely believe his eyes. A little girl stood on the steps, looking almost wraithlike in the whirling snow.

Mitchell could see that the child was thinly dressed. She clutched a ragged shawl around her thin shoulders, and her eyes were huge and pleading.

"Come in, child," said Dr. Mitchell, but the little girl shook her head.

"My mother is very sick." Her voice was as thin as she was. "Please come and help her."

"Haven't you a regular doctor?" Dr. Mitchell asked. "I'm a neurologist, not a general practitioner."

"You must come," the child repeated. "My mother wants you."

Dr. Mitchell felt he was no match for the child's desperate eyes. "At least come in and wait until I get dressed," he told her, but the child remained on the snow-covered steps in the open doorway. Mitchell shrugged and went upstairs to dress.

As the doctor trudged after the child through the snow, he often lost sight of his small guide. At times she seemed to vanish into the storm, merging with the whirling snow. But each time he stopped in bewilderment, she would reappear at his side and take his hand.

"This way," she would whisper. "This way."

At last they came to a house in a poor section of the city. The child tugged open the front door and beckoned the doctor inside. "Go upstairs, please."

As he ran up the steps, Dr. Mitchell glanced back. His small guide was gone, he noted in annoyance. But he had no difficulty in finding his patient. The upper floor was nothing but a garret. Huddled under ragged quilts on the bed, a woman lay coughing desperately.

"Dr. Mitchell!" the woman gasped in surprise. "Thank God you've come. But how did you know I was sick?"

Mitchell didn't answer. He was staring in astonishment at the woman, for he recognized her. Some years before, she had been a servant in his home. But he had no time to puzzle over this strange coincidence, for it was obvious that the woman was very ill with pneumonia. He set about at once to do what he could for her. By morning he felt that at last she was out of danger.

"Now, my dear, I think we should talk," he told her. "When I came in, you asked me how I knew you were sick. But you yourself had sent your little daughter for me. You have a very intelligent and brave child — and a very determined one. She wouldn't take no for an answer. By the way, I wonder where she has got to. She didn't come upstairs with me."

The woman's eyes filled with tears. "I don't understand, Doctor. My daughter died a month ago. All I have left to remember her by are those clothes hanging on that peg over there."

With a sense of wonderment, Dr. Mitchell walked across the room. Hanging from the peg was the thin dress he had seen the child wearing, and the ragged shawl. He touched them with trembling fingers, and found they were dry. With a sinking heart, he looked down at his own clothing. It was still wet from the storm through which he had been led by the child.

The Wandering Coffins
of Barbados

On the surface, the West Indian island of Barbados is a smiling, sunlit place. But under the surface, beneath the ground, a strange tumult seems to have been going on for over a century. It would appear that the dead of Barbados do not always lie quietly in their coffins.

Take, for example, the tomb of Sir Evan Mc-Gregor. It is a stone crypt carved of native rock. Four feet of the crypt rise above the ground. The rest is sunk four feet below the earth.

Sir Evan was entombed there in 1841. But on August 24, 1943, men came to open the tomb and disturb his rest. It wasn't an easy task, for it involved breaking seals, prying off a heavy door-sized slab, and then tearing out the bricks that covered the entrance to the vault.

Why the break-in by the gang of sweating workmen? They had been hired by a group of Freemasons who wanted to enter the tomb to pay their respects to Alexander Irvine, whose body happened to share the crypt with Sir Evan. Irvine was the founder of Freemasonry in Barbados.

As the bricks were loosened and removed, a workman's chisel struck metal. More bricks came away, making a hole through which the workmen could see. They peered in and gasped in astonishment. A lead-sheathed coffin was standing on end against the other side of the bricked entrance!

Uneasily, the workmen looked at each other. They estimated the coffin's weight at about 600 pounds. How could it have been moved from its slab across the vault to be upended against the entrance? But the Freemasons urged them to go on with their work. They took out the rest of the bricks and eased the coffin onto the floor.

Once inside the crypt, the group received another shock. Where was the coffin of Alexander Irvine?

It was not in the vault — no doubt about that! Yet witnesses had seen Irvine's remains laid beside Sir Evan's when the tomb was sealed and bricked up in 1841. Somehow Irvine's coffin had vanished, and Sir Evan's had moved a distance of twenty feet!

The news of the disturbed tomb brought first

the police, then interested scientists to the scene. All agreed that the tomb had not been opened between 1841 and 1943. But neither group could offer a solution to the mystery. Sir Evan's coffin was restored to its proper niche and the tomb was closed again. To this day, no one has yet figured out what became of the remains of Alexander Irvine.

The Chase vault, near Christ Church on another part of Barbados, has also been the scene of strange goings-on. The vault received its first coffin, that of a Mrs. Goddard, in 1807. In the next two years several other family members were entombed there. In 1809 the tomb was sealed shut with a heavy capstone over the entrance.

In 1812 the vault was again opened for the entombment of another member of the Chase family. But the condition of the vault sent the mourners into hysterics.

The big, lead-sheathed coffins, so heavy that it took eight men to lift each of them, were no longer in their niches. Instead, they lay helter-skelter all over the vault's brick floor, as if tossed there by a giant's hand.

One coffin, containing the remains of Thomas Chase, stood upside down opposite the shelf on which it had originally rested. Only two coffins were still in their proper places. One was that containing Mrs. Goddard's remains. The other belonged to her baby granddaughter.

Shocked, the family ordered the coffins put back where they belonged. They then had a stone slab placed over the vault's entrance — a slab so heavy that six men had to push it into place. Seals were placed on the entrance.

Years passed, and death claimed another Chase. The tomb was unsealed and another shambles met the outraged eyes of the family! Coffins lay all over the place. Again, only those of Mrs. Goddard and her granddaughter rested in their original niches.

Wearily, the family ordered the tomb restored to order. The coffins were put back in place. Once more a heavy stone was rolled over the entrance and seals placed upon it. But this time the Chases took an added precaution. They hired armed guards to stand outside the vault day and night.

In 1819 the vault was opened to receive the body of Thomasina Clark. The same crazy disorder had taken over again. Coffins were tumbled about the floor. Others stood on end against the walls or rested on their sides in corners.

Lord Combermere, Governor of Barbados, was present. "The dead have a right to lie in peace," he proclaimed angrily. This time he took the precaution of personally sealing up the vault after having the floor covered with fine sand. "If vandals enter the crypt, they will have to leave footmarks!"

One year later Lord Combermere broke the seals. The heavy entrance stone was dragged away, and the witnesses peered inside. Not a single footprint showed on the sand-covered floor. But again the coffins were strewn carelessly about.

"There will be no more burials here," announced Lord Combermere. He ordered the Chase family to have their dead removed and buried elsewhere. The vault was to remain empty forever.

But on the heavy stone that covers its entrance, someone has carved a huge question mark.

The Horror in the Gray House

Ghosts aren't always found in old castles or deserted mansions. Sometimes they turn up in ordinary neighborhoods, like yours or mine. Take the gray frame house in Detroit, Michigan, for example. It's just an ordinary, pleasant-looking house in a quiet neighborhood — a house that could be said to have no personality at all. But no one wants to live in that house anymore. The owner doesn't even want to rent it. Why?

The last tenants could tell you the answer. They were Lillian and Bill Adams. They rented the house because it was close to Bill's job.

Bill Adams worked a night shift and had to sleep during the day. For that reason, he decided to move into the small back bedroom. "It was in a quiet part of the house, where I wouldn't be disturbed by the sounds of children playing, or traffic.

"I had used the back room for about a week when I began to have horrible nightmares. These dreams were so real that I'd wake up limp with fear! I'd find myself sitting up in bed, screaming so that my throat was sore.

"In one of the dreams, I opened a door and a horribly-disfigured body fell out. Things got so bad that I told my wife I'd have to go to a psychiatrist if the dreams didn't stop."

The dreams did stop because Bill moved out of the back room. Life in the Adams household settled down to an easygoing, peaceful routine. Then Bill's grandmother came to stay for a few days.

"Because the back bedroom was the only spare room, we put her in there," Bill remembers. "I didn't mention my nightmares to her — in fact, I had almost forgotten them. But the next morning my grandmother showed up at breakfast, pale and shaky. She said she hadn't been able to sleep at all because all night she heard noises as though someone were trying to claw his way into the room. Yet each time she turned on the light, there was nothing to be seen. She decided to cut short her stay and go back home."

By this time the Adams had decided there was something very wrong with the back bedroom, but they avoided discussing it. The room stayed empty until Patterson, Bill's cousin, stopped by on his way to the West Coast. To save the expense of a hotel, he asked if he could sleep in the back room.

To this day, Patterson says he has never forgotten his first and only night in that room.

"I didn't know anything about the place. My cousin hadn't discussed it, and there was no reason for me to be afraid. It was the night of October 27, and Bill went off to work shortly before midnight. I decided to retire a few minutes later.

"I had lain there facing the wall for just a few minutes — when something turned me over! Don't ask me to describe the feeling. All I know is that something rolled me over so I faced the bedroom door. A woman was standing there with her back to me!

"At first I thought it was Lillian, but then I saw that the woman seemed much older and she had long gray hair hanging down her back. She had on a fur coat; a blue dress showed below it.

"For some reason I began to shake. I wanted her to turn around so I could see her face — but at the same time I was afraid to see it. Then I thought she spoke to me without turning, in a kind of hissing voice. She seemed to be saying, 'Come here. Come here.'

"I felt as though I was being pulled out of the bed toward her, and I screamed as loud as I could — and every light in the house went out!"

In the dark, Patterson knew that no matter what happened, he had to get out of that room. He ran into the kitchen where he bumped into

Lillian Adams, who had heard him scream. Suddenly the lights went on again.

At that moment, according to Mrs. Adams, a horrible wailing sound came from the back room. "I have never heard anything like it in my life. It literally seemed to make our hair stand on end. Then there was a terrible, sickening smell and the door to the back room opened and closed with a bang."

Thoroughly frightened, Mrs. Adams called the police. They searched the house and yard, but found nothing. When Bill Adams came home, Lillian and Patterson told him about their experience.

"I still couldn't believe there were such things as ghosts," says Bill Adams, "but I suspected somebody was trying to scare us out of the house for reasons we didn't understand. I decided to set a trap for whoever it was. I'd spend the rest of the night in the back room, pretending to sleep — but ready to grab the first joker who showed up!"

Bill Adams went into the little room and lay down on the bed, leaving the door open. From where he lay he could see Lillian and Patterson sitting in the lighted front room. The back room was dim, but enough light came through the door so that he could make out objects.

"I was getting drowsy, when I heard a sound in the room. I thought it was Lillian, and I started to tell her to stay in the front room so I could get this thing settled once and for all.

"I turned over to look — and saw an old woman's face just a few inches from mine! The eyes were staring past me, and the mouth was moving as if she was trying to talk. But no words came out, only a hissing sound. Then a terrible stench seemed to spread through the room!"

How he got to the front room, Bill Adams doesn't remember. He was almost hysterical with fear, but his description of the thing he had seen reminded Patterson of the woman who had appeared to him.

"Was she wearing a blue dress and a fur coat?" Patterson asked. Bill shook his head. He had only seen the face, and the memory of it made him shudder.

Lillian was staring at Patterson. "I have a blue dress and a fur coat," she said. She went to her closet and pulled them out.

"Those are the clothes the old woman wore!" said Patterson in astonishment.

Suddenly Lillian dropped the garments. A ghastly smell had begun to seep from them — the same smell that had sent Bill running from the back bedroom.

This was the last straw. The Adamses decided they would not spend another night in the gray house. They packed up and left in the morning, after arranging to stay with Lillian's sister, Virginia, and her husband, Leo.

Virginia was skeptical about their story. "Probably a rat died behind the wall, and that accounts for the smell. The rest just has to be imagination." That evening she and Leo went to the gray house to investigate.

"Leo was laughing about Bill's spook," said

Lillian. "He said, 'I think I'll make the lady's acquaintance.' He went into the back bedroom and lay down on the bed. Then I heard him give a terrible groan. He came running out, as white as a sheet. But he couldn't tell me what had happened, just grabbed my hand and dragged me out of that house."

When the owner of the house heard his tenants' story, he asked the police to go over it from top to bottom. Nothing was found to account for the smell — not even a dead rat.

Was it a ghost that appeared in the back bedroom? If so, why did she put on Lillian's dress and coat? These are questions that still puzzle Lillian and Bill Adams — questions for which there are no answers so far.

Today the gray house stands empty and boarded up. Strangely enough, many people have asked to rent it for the night so they could sleep in the back bedroom. But the owner has refused all such requests. The house, he feels, is better left empty — except for the thing that haunts the back bedroom.

The Child Who Wanted to Go Home

Harold Lothridge was a man with more common sense than imagination. Perhaps that was just as well, for he was a carpenter who dealt in down-to-earth items like nails, boards, and tools. No one was more surprised than Harold when he had a vision that solved a murder.

It happened shortly after Harold and his wife had gone to bed. Harold seemed to be dropping off, but suddenly he sat bolt upright, shuddering.

"I saw her!" he gasped when his wife turned on the light. "I saw Dorothy Schneider, that little girl who was murdered up near Mount Morris last week. I heard her saying, 'I want to go home! I want to go home!'"

"It must have been a nightmare . . ." his wife began.

"No!" Harold insisted. "It was real. I saw him kill her and throw her out of the car — a robin's-egg blue sedan."

"You saw the man who murdered her?" his wife breathed.

Harold gulped and nodded. "It was Adolph Hotelling!"

The couple looked at each other in blank astonishment. They knew Hotelling well. He was the Deacon of the church they attended in Mount Morris, Michigan. They couldn't imagine a respectable man like Deacon Hotelling being mixed up in a murder.

But Harold insisted that it was the Deacon he had seen in his vision. His wife tried to talk him out of the idea. How could the Deacon be the killer of five-year-old Dorothy Schneider? She begged Harold to forget this fantastic notion.

But Harold could not forget. He brooded about it all through breakfast. Then he went to see his father, and told him about the vision. "Don't tell another soul," said the older man. "You could get into trouble saying things like that about a man like Hotelling."

Harold, however, was in no mood to follow this advice. He felt a compulsion to settle the matter, to somehow prove he was right. It was either that, or admit he was crazy. In the end he decided to take his story to the county sheriff.

"Sounds to me like you must have had a couple of drinks too many," suggested the sheriff.

"I don't drink," said Harold stubbornly.

"Well, I don't think I ever saw the Deacon driving a blue car. But I can see you're upset. I'll tell you what I'll do. Just to put your mind at rest, you can go over to Hotelling's house with a couple of my deputies."

When Hotelling heard about Harold's vision, he laughed. "Do you mean to tell me you're serious? You had a nightmare, Harold — probably caused by a heavy dinner. Besides, I drive a black car. Come on out in the garage and see for yourself."

Hotelling led Harold and the deputies to the garage. There, just as he had said, stood a black car.

"Sorry, Mr. Hotelling," one of the deputies began — then stopped because his signet ring had just scraped against the car's fender. He held up the ring for the others to see. Flecks of black paint, mixed with flecks of blue paint, stuck to it. The scratch upon the fender showed that under the black paint, the car's color was *robin's-egg blue!*

Hotelling stood in stunned silence for a moment, then broke down completely. "I did it!" he sobbed. "I killed Dorothy Schneider. Thank God you've found out, for I haven't been able to sleep since it happened. I keep dreaming that I hear her crying, 'I want to go home! I want to go home!'"

Hotelling was sentenced to life imprisonment in 1928 for his crime. Harold, whose vision had brought him to justice, believed that Hotelling wanted to be caught.

"Do you remember that Sunday after Dorothy's body was found?" he asked his wife. "Do you remember how Deacon Hotelling stood up in church and prayed out loud? He told us, 'I have asked God to help us find this child's killer, and he has promised me help.' Well, perhaps the help Hotelling asked for came to me in that vision."

VIP Ghosts

Movie actress Anne Francis lives in a haunted house. It doesn't frighten her, because she says that ghosts can't really harm the living.

The house is in the Brentwood section of Los Angeles, California. Anne lives there with her two daughters, Jane, 11, and Margaret, three. The girls don't seem to mind the ghosts any more than their mother does.

"I believe something tragic or violent happened in the house at one time," says Anne. "I was in the living room one day when my dog Smoke came running in, as though he was chasing something. I couldn't see anything, but I knew he could because he was so upset. So I closed my eyes and tried to open my mind to whatever was going on. Then I sensed a man wearing blue work clothes, with a wrench in his hand. He seemed to be threatening another man. Then the impression was gone, and Smoke stopped growling.

"On another occasion, a loud banging began in Margaret's room. No one was there, but it sounded as though something was trying to knock the house down.

"I have often heard footsteps going past me. At other times, a clicking sound will start first in one part of the house, then in another. A rocking chair in my bedroom often begins to rock back and forth all by itself."

Audrey Meadows is another actress who believes she has met a ghost. It happened several years ago when Audrey shared a room with a friend named Mary in a house in Montclair, New Jersey.

The room was on the second floor. It must have once belonged to a child, because there were children's books in the bookcase.

The first night Audrey and Mary spent there was hot, so they opened the window wide. The next morning they found it closed and locked when they woke up.

The same thing happened the next night, and the next. "I'll bet the landlady sneaks in and closes it when we're asleep," said Mary. But when questioned, the landlady indignantly denied coming into their room. To make sure that she didn't, however, Mary pushed a heavy chest of drawers in front of the door the next night before going to bed.

In the morning the door was still blocked by

the chest of drawers—but the window was again closed and locked.

The next night Audrey had an idea. She got a heavy block of wood and wedged the window open. Now it couldn't close by itself.

When the girls awakened, the window was locked shut, and the block of wood lay on the chest of drawers. Audrey's eye was also caught by one of the books which had been pulled halfway out of the bookcases. It was a copy of *Black Beauty*.

The girls were completely bewildered. What did it all mean? The window continued to be found shut each morning, and the copy of the book was found in a different place, day after day.

Finally Audrey decided to discuss the room with the landlady. Whose room had it been? What was its history?

To her surprise, the woman began to cry. "It was my son's room," she admitted. "He died there last year of pneumonia. He was only twelve."

"Then the book was his?" asked Audrey.

"Yes. *Black Beauty* was his favorite story."

To Audrey, the whole thing seemed suddenly clear. "I think that your son must come back to the room each night to read the book. That's why we find it in a different place each morning. And the window—he closes it because, being sick, he was afraid of the drafts."

The girls remained in the house for the rest of the summer, confident that the child's ghost meant them no harm. "People think ghosts are

119

always evil, but that's wrong," she says with a smile. "Ghosts can be very nice people!"

Even Audrey might find it hard to describe the ghost that haunts the Mackenzie house as "nice," however.

The house was the home of William Lyon Mackenzie, the first mayor of the city of Toronto, Canada. Mackenzie died there in 1861, and the house is now preserved as a national monument. The only problem is getting caretakers who will consent to live there.

The last caretakers were Mr. and Mrs. Alex Dobban. They considered themselves lucky when they saw the spacious apartment on the top floor. It was to be theirs, rent-free, as long as they took care of the house and showed visitors around it.

The Dobbans moved into the Mackenzie homestead in April 1960. In May they moved out.

"It was the noises," explained Alex Dobban. "All night long, footsteps would tramp up and down the stairs — and there wouldn't be a soul there. Mr. Mackenzie had installed a printing press in the basement during his last years, and it would start up by itself, even though the room it was kept in was locked. And then there was the piano in the front parlor. One night it began to play — if that's what you call it. The racket it made sounded just like a child hitting the keys with clenched fists!"

If the Dobbans had met the Edmunds, they might not have moved in at all. The Edmunds had preceded them as caretakers. They had stayed on the job for three turbulent years. It took the phantom of a woman to drive them out!

"I woke up one night, and saw a woman standing at the head of the bed, leaning over me," reported Mrs. Edmunds. "The bed was pushed against the wall, so it wasn't really possible for anyone to stand there like that. She stood staring at me for a moment, then she leaned over and her long hair brushed my face. I screamed, and she vanished."

Mrs. Edmunds and the long-haired ghost met again a few months later. "Her hair brushing my face woke me. This time, however, she reached out and hit me. I had a black eye for days!"

The strain of living and working in the Mackenize homestead made the Edmunds look rather ghostly themselves. Both lost a great deal of weight, and they became pale and nervous. The ghostly woman did not reappear, but a man took her place.

"He was a small man, wearing a frock coat and side whiskers," says Mr. Edmunds. "My wife saw him in our bedroom, and I saw him myself in the parlor. He looked something like the portrait of Mackenzie, except that Mackenzie was bald, and the ghost had a full head of hair. Then I learned that Mackenzie used to wear a wig in public — so perhaps the ghost was his."

The black eye she received — and the over-watering of her plants — were the two things that finally made Mrs. Edmunds decide that she and her husband must leave. "I had my plants locked up in a room off the kitchen. Often those last months I'd come down and find them soaking with water. There would be water spilled all over, and mud on the curtains. I think that woman did it out of spite."

The goings-on at the Mackenzie homestead aroused the curiosity of Andy MacFarlane, a reporter on the *Toronto Telegram*. He decided there might be a story in the old place, and in June 1960 he arranged to spend a night there alone. In the morning he reported that not a ghostly sound or appearance had disturbed him.

The Edmunds and the Dobbans were not reassured by MacFarlane's experience. As far as they were concerned, the Mackenzie homestead was haunted.

Since then, however, no one has complained of restless spirits in the old house. The Edmunds think they know the reason why. They point out that on July 1, 1960, Archdeacon John Frank of the Holy Trinity Church in Toronto went to the homestead and read prayers to drive the ghosts away.

Landing on a Strange Planet

Patrolman Lonnie Zamora is as sensible a man as you might meet. He isn't given to flights of fancy, and doesn't care for science fiction. His neighbors in Socorro, New Mexico, will vouch for the fact that Zamora isn't one to let imagination hinder him in the performance of his duty.

On April 24, 1964, Zamora was cruising along the highway when an uncommon thing happened. There was a roaring sound, and a blue glow lit up the sky overhead. Then the glow seemed to rush toward desert gullies to the south.

Could it be one of those jet planes in trouble? Zamora wondered. He didn't waste time speculating on the whyfor of the blue glow in broad daylight, but swung his car around and sped off toward the gullies.

123

It couldn't be a plane crash, Zamora decided as he bumped along over the rough ground. There had been no explosion, no smoke — Zamora jammed on his brakes! He had just crested a rise in the sand. Now he sat frozen in astonishment, unable to believe what he saw 400 feet ahead.

The air was full of dust — but the thing in front of him was quite plain. It was a white object, about 15 feet high, and egg-shaped. Figures in light-colored clothing were moving about the object.

"They were people, all right," Zamora swears. "Little people, no bigger than children. I couldn't make out their features, but they weren't any little green men out of a science-fiction movie."

Something told Zamora to be very, very quiet. He moved his car carefully back until it was in the shadow of the next mesa. From this point, he could still keep an eye on the strange object and the tiny figures around it.

Keeping his voice low, he called Sergeant Sam Chavez of the state police over his car radio. But the few minutes it took for Chavez to get there were too many. An ear-splitting roar flung Zamora to the ground. Raising his head, he saw the egg-shaped object rising into the air on a pillar of blue flame. It hovered, then swung to the southwest and vanished from sight.

Shakily Zamora got to his feet. Chavez was just driving up. Expressionless, the trooper listened to Zamora's story. Then he went with Zamora to the spot where the egg-shaped object had rested.

In his report Chavez noted that "burned grass was still smoking. We found four wedge-shaped depressions about four inches in depth that might have been made by landing gear."

The next to investigate were specialists from the Air Force. They checked out the site, and checked into Zamora's reputation. They found out what everyone in his hometown already knew — Patrolman Zamora was a solid citizen and a good policeman.

In due time, the Air Force issued their report. Patrolman Zamora, it stated, had indeed seen an unknown flying object.

The Dream That Saved a Life

The night of August 15, 1951, was hot and still in Chicago. John Dolan put off going to bed as long as possible because he was sure the heat would make it difficult to sleep. Finally he gave in and got into bed. He lay there thinking about the trip he had to make to Detroit the next day — a trip he made regularly twice a week as a consultant to an automobile company.

As he drifted into sleep, Dolan dreamed he was on the train he regularly took to Detroit, sitting in the seat he always reserved. A woman sat beside him with a child on her lap. Across the aisle was a man reading a newspaper.

Suddenly there was a terrible grinding crash. A shock ran through the train. Somehow Dolan knew it had run into another locomotive on the same track. In his dream he could see the crushed coaches up ahead plunging over an embankment. He could hear screams, shouts, and groans coming from the injured caught in the twisted wreckage.

He turned to the woman beside him to warn her to get down on the floor with the child. But it was too late. The car he was in shuddered and tipped over the embankment. He felt himself flung through a window, plunging into darkness through broken glass. . . .

Dolan wrenched himself awake. His groans had awakened his wife. Trembling, he told her about the nightmare. "It was so real, so real," he kept saying.

The next morning, he still felt depressed and weighed down by the memory of the dream.

"Perhaps you should take it seriously, if it bothers you so," his wife suggested. "Why don't you telephone the company in Detroit and tell them you're going to take a later train?"

Dolan thought it over, and decided to follow her advice. He reserved space on a train leaving that evening. When he got to the railway station he decided to buy a newspaper. But as he reached for the paper his heart seemed to stop for a second.

Train Wreck Outside Chicago! screamed the headline.

Dolan read the story with a sinking feeling of having seen it all before. The train he would have taken had crashed into another, just as his dream had foretold. A number of people had been killed when the cars they were in hurtled over the embankment. Others had been seriously injured.

Dolan cancelled his trip and went to the scene of the wreck. He stood on the embankment, staring down at the crushed coaches and wrecked engines. The dream had saved his life — but he felt no relief. Instead, an overpowering sense of guilt and remorse flooded through him. Who was the passenger who had taken the seat he usually occupied? he wondered. Who had died in his place?

Although his wife and friends tried to talk him out of it, Dolan could not shake off this feeling in the days to come. He agreed that he was lucky to be alive, but he couldn't help wondering whether his escape had cost another's life. He went to the railway company and began to make inquiries about the passenger who had taken the seat he usually reserved.

It took some time, but finally the company officials agreed to give him the information.

When Dolan cancelled his reservation, a young architect named Frank Mysal had taken the seat on the train. Mysal had been thrown through the train window in the wreck and killed. He left a wife and two children.

Dolan's conscience would not let him rest. He sold off property and put the money in a letter which he sent to Mysal's wife. A note went with the money.

"Your husband died for me," the note said.

The Thing

"I can't explain the Thing," says Arthur Shuttlewood, editor of the *Warminister Journal.* "I can only say that it came to my town of Warminister on Christmas Day 1965, and it came to terrorize us!"

Warminister is a quiet town in southern England. It sees few strangers from year to year, and it had never before seen anything like the Thing!

The Thing made its first appearance at 6:15 A.M. on December 25. Mrs. Madge Blye was on her way to early morning service at the church. "Suddenly I heard a weird crackling above my head, accompanied by a high-pitched whine," she remembers.

Before Mrs. Blye could even wonder about the source of the sound, she was picked up by an unseen force and hurled against the church wall.

"I felt as if I were pinned there by invisible fingers. My arms and neck were freezing as though gripped by icy hands. Then blows began to rain down on my head. People heard me screaming and ran out of the church. Then whatever it was just let me fall to the ground."

A few minutes later, the Thing reached a house on the other side of town. There a young girl was awakened by the whimpering and barking of her dog, tied in the garden outside. She went down and opened the door to see what was bothering her pet — and an unseen fist knocked her down! At the same time, she too heard the weird, crackling sound.

"What seemed to be an icy sponge pressed hard on the back of my neck," reported the girl. "My head was jerked forward and down. I struggled and screamed, and finally managed to free myself and crawl into the house!"

Next, Warminister's head postmaster was awakened by a banging on the roof over his head.

"The ceiling shook. It sounded as though all the tiles were being yanked off by some terrific force. Then my wife and I heard a frantic, scrambling sound overhead as if someone were hurriedly putting all the tiles back in place. Throughout all the commotion, there was also a funny crackling sound."

The postmaster and his wife ran out into the yard. Nothing and no one was to be seen on the roof. The tiles were all where they should be.

For nine more months, the Thing kept up its antics. Day after day, indignant, frightened citizens reported being punched, knocked down, and kept awake at night by thunderous clattering and banging noises. The crackling sound put everyone's nerves on edge.

Was the Thing responsible for the flock of pigeons who all plummeted to earth, dead on impact? A biologist, Dr. David Holton, gathered up the dead birds and took them to his laboratory for examination. What he discovered seemed to make no sense.

"I don't know what caused those birds to fall out of the sky like that, but I do know that almost instant rigor mortis set in. I examined them very shortly after they hit the ground, and I can testify to their rigid condition. As I'm sure most people know it normally takes hours for rigor mortis to set in."

The citizens of Warminister held a public inquiry to try to find an explanation for the Thing. More than 600 people attended. A few blamed the disturbances on "unidentified pranksters." But those who had been pummeled and knocked down by something they couldn't see pointed out indignantly that the so-called pranksters were not only unidentified, but invisible!

One man suggested that the Thing might really be the result of "experiments in nearby government laboratories and military establishments." But the government was ready for that. They replied that no such experiments were going on in their installations, and no new weapons or aircraft were being tested.

No new aircraft! The people of Warminister

had cause to remember that point when they heard about the experience of the Reverend Graham Phillips, vicar of the nearby town of Heytesbury.

The Reverend Phillips had been out walking in the evening with his wife and children.

"Suddenly we heard this peculiar droning, crackling noise. Then over Warminister a brightly glowing object appeared. It moved back and forth, hovering over the town for about twenty minutes. Then it vanished."

Soon other reports came in from other neighboring towns about a strange, glowing object seen over Warminister. Some reports described the object as "cigar-shaped." Others claimed it was "circular." All agreed that it was big and glowing.

Oddly enough, no one in Warminister ever seems to have spotted it. They were wondering what had happened to the Thing. After nine months, the town was strangely quiet. They nursed their bruises and tried to relax.

Warminister is still quiet, but Arthur Shuttlewood wonders how long it will last. "I talked with too many reliable, sensible citizens who were terrorized by the Thing not to be convinced that something very strange went on in this town. I'm not too sure the story is over yet. True, the Thing seems to be gone — but who knows whether it might not decide to return and torment us again?"

The Forest of
Vanishing Children

The Angeles National Forest spreads over 690,000 rugged acres in Southern California. It is a mountain wilderness, studded with towering peaks — beautiful, beckoning, and sinister. Every year thousands of people seeking relaxation flock to it. Some of them never return.

In the last few years four children have vanished in the Angeles Forest. They have disappeared as completely as though the forest had gulped them down. Although search parties made up of lawmen, forest rangers, mountaineers, and volunteers have combed the area, not a trace of the four young people has been found.

The first to vanish were Donald Baker, 13, and his friend, Brenda Howell, 11. When last seen on August 5, 1956, the two were riding their bicycles in the direction of the San Gabriel Reservoir in the forest.

By evening, neither Donald nor Brenda had returned. Their parents called the police.

Near the reservoir, the searchers found Brenda's bicycle and Donald's sweater. Had the children fallen into the reservoir? Navy divers were called in, but a search of the mile-long stretch of water revealed nothing.

The police broadcast pleas for any information anyone might have. A woman called to say that Brenda and Donald had passed her house on August 5th at 4:30 P.M. on their bicycles. According to a service station attendant in Azusa, they had ridden by his station at 8:30 P.M. These were the only leads.

The search went on for weeks. Brenda and Donald are still missing.

Almost a year later, on March 23, 1957, the Angeles Forest reached out for another victim. Eight-year-old Tommy Bowman was hiking there with his family. The Bowmans were on a trail near the Arroyo Seco Ranger Station.

Tommy liked to be first. He broke impatiently away from the group and ran ahead. "I can beat you all!" he called back as he rounded a turn in the trail. A few minutes later, the rest of the group reached the turn — but Tommy was nowhere to be seen!

Again a full-scale search went into action. This time, not only patrols of people scoured the area, but helicopters and dogs got in on the action. Not a crevice, crag, or cave was left unexamined. But Tommy was gone. He has never been found.

After that, things were quiet in the forest —

for three years. But on July 13, 1960, another child vanished!

It happened at a YMCA camp. Seven-year-old Bruce Kremen had started out on a hike with the other boys, but he seemed to tire quickly. The group leader thought he might not be feeling well, so he walked him back until the camp grounds were in sight.

The leader stood watching until he saw that Bruce was only a few yards from the camp. Then he went back to where the other boys waited, and resumed the hike.

Later, in the evening, the hikers returned to camp. They learned an astonishing fact. No one at the camp had seen Bruce return! And Bruce was nowhere to be found in the camp area!

This time the search lasted twelve days. Inch by inch, three hundred trained men went over a ten-square-mile area around the camp. The result was zero. Not even a shred of Bruce's clothing was found.

Since Bruce disappeared, new regulations have gone into effect in the forest to make sure no more children disappear. Forest rangers and camp personnel keep a close watch. No children are allowed in the forest unless accompanied by an adult.

The precautions seem to be working. Bruce was the last child to be lost in the Angeles Forest. But what happened to Bruce and the other three young people? Only the brooding forest knows the answer to that question.

The Ghost Dog

In 1897 Ed Jacques rode out to the foothills of the Kiamichi Mountains in Oklahoma, looking for work. New settlers had moved into the area, and he hoped that some of them might have use for his services as a hired hand.

As he moved into the foothills, he passed an old Indian cemetery. Not far from it was a tumbledown log cabin, obviously abandoned. Its battered door swung to and fro on creaking hinges in the wind.

Ed's spirits lifted as he caught sight, about a half mile on, of a large log farmhouse, with well maintained barns and fences. Mr. Matthews, the owner of this spread, proved hospitable. He invited Ed to spend the night, and said he knew where work was to be found.

"There's a man named Brady, who lives on

the other side of the old graveyard. He settled there a year ago, but he hasn't had any luck getting hired help. Last year he hired three different men, but none of them stayed longer than a month. Why don't you ride over tomorrow morning and see if he can use you?"

The next day Ed took Matthews' advice. Brady put him to work at once, and said the job was his as long as he cared to stay. Ed rode over every morning to the Brady place, and back again every evening to spend the night at the Matthews house.

"Things went on peacefully this way for a couple of weeks. Then one morning, as I neared the old cemetery, I saw a black and white fox terrier come trotting out of the cemetery. As I rode past, it suddenly leaped up and landed on the horse behind my saddle."

Startled, Ed grabbed his quirt and lashed out at the dog to frighten him off the horse. But the quirt only whistled through empty air.

Puzzled, Ed swung around in his saddle. "I could see the dog crouched there still. I reached around to pull it off — and grabbed a handful of empty air! I couldn't feel it, but the dog was still there."

Digging in his spurs, Ed urged his horse to a gallop. Surely the terrier would fall off. But it continued to cling to the horse — until Ed reached the Brady place. Then it disappeared.

Had he imagined the animal? Ed wondered. But two evenings later, he met it again at the cemetery. And again it leaped up behind him on the horse, and rode to the Matthews house on his bedroll. From then on it appeared to hitch a ride with him about twice a week.

Oddly enough, Ed says he felt no fear of his strange companion. "It didn't seem to mean me any harm. In a way, we became pals."

Still, he said nothing about the dog to either the Matthews or the Bradys. "But I did notice that they had begun to eye me as if they expected me to say something!"

Finally Mr. Matthews asked him, "Have you noticed a fox terrier riding on your bedroll sometimes?"

Astonished, Ed replied, "You mean you've seen it?"

"Of course. Brady's seen him too. Aren't you afraid of him?"

"No," said Ed thoughtfully. "After the first time, when I found out he wasn't real, I stopped being scared. But I've wondered why he appears to me."

"Well, you're not the first stranger around here to have Foxy as a passenger, but you're the first he hasn't scared away. Foxy was the reason those other hired hands of Brady's quit."

Then Matthews told Ed the story of Foxy. Three years before, an old man named Jacobs had come to the foothills to homestead. "Riding behind him on his bedroll was Foxy, very much alive then. All Jacobs had to say was, 'Jump up, Foxy,' and the little dog would jump up on the horse."

Jacobs had moved into what was now the tumbledown cabin that Ed had noticed near the graveyard. Then one winter evening he had caught a chill. Pneumonia set in, and Jacobs died a few days later.

"When the old man breathed his last, Foxy ran out the cabin door and headed for the cemetery," said Matthews. "He seemed to know that we would be bringing his master there. We dug a grave the next morning, and Foxy stood at the head of it, watching us. Then he lay down by the grave, and stayed there, no matter how much I coaxed. We brought him food, but he wouldn't eat. We carried him to our house, but he always ran back to the grave. He stayed there by the grave until he died of grief.

"About a year ago Foxy showed up again, riding on the bedroll of the first fellow Brady hired. It seems that when a stranger rides past the graveyard, Foxy comes back to see if it's Jacobs. You're the first friend the poor little ghost has found."

When winter came, Ed left the foothills. He never returned, but he told the story to a number of people. To his friends he often said, "I wonder if Foxy is still hitching rides at Kiamichi? I wonder if he's found anyone yet who will say, 'Jump up, Foxy!'"

The Photographic Mind of Ted Serios

A small thin man sat in a Chicago hotel room. In his hands he held a Polaroid camera loaded with fresh film. He held the camera at arm's lengh and stared into the lens for two or three minutes, concentrating until the veins stood out on his forehead. Then he carefully clicked the shutter.

Dr. Jule Eisenbud, of the University of Colorado, took the camera. The print he pulled from it was dim and blurry, but it was a picture of a skyscraper.

Incredible, thought Dr. Eisenbud, but it was true! The thin man, whose name was Ted Serios, had caused the picture of the skyscraper to appear on the film simply by thinking it! He ordered Serios to perform this feat again.

This time the print produced showed a hotel front, with the named *Stevens* over the door. Eisenbud knew about the Stevens Hotel. It had burned down years ago.

In great excitement Eisenbud wrote about the test of Serios' abilities to a friend. "I am trying to show that we all have the ability to do what Ted Serios did — if only we could discover how to develop and use this ability."

Dr. Eisenbud called Ted Serios' strange talent "precognition." But precognition means the ability to perceive something before it happens. Perhaps Ted's ability to think pictures onto a roll of film should be called a kind of telepathy — the ability to receive or send thoughts. Ted was able to transfer mental images from his mind to film.

Dr. Eisenbud felt that other scientists should see what Ted could do. But when he offered to have Ted perform for them, little interest was shown! Some had even seen Serios do his mental photography — but their attitude seemed to be, "So what?"

"I watched a demonstration with Serios," one scientist told Eisenbud, "but I wasn't impressed. I suggested some buildings to him, but he got the wrong buildings on the prints. So I just lost interest."

Dr. Eisenbud found it hard to believe that the scientist failed to see how marvelous it was that Serios could actually think an image of a building onto film — no matter what building! No one denied that Serios could perform this incredible feat. Why, then, was no one interested?

Was it because Serios was an alcoholic? Alcoholics are known to be unreliable. Was this the reason that mention of his name seemed to turn off those scientists?

Dr. Eisenbud was inclined to believe he had part of the explanation. He suspected that the rest of the reason lay in Serios' former association with the ghost of the pirate Jean Lafitte.

Lafitte's ghost and Serios had gotten together in 1953, years before Dr. Eisenbud became interested. At that time Serios was a bellhop in a Chicago hotel. One day a fellow employee named George Johannes offered to try to hypnotize Serios. It proved surprisingly easy. Serios went into a deep trance almost at once, and in the trance he seemed to be holding a conversation with the spirit of Lafitte, a notorious pirate and smuggler of the 19th century.

Under hypnosis, Serios said that Lafitte had told him where he had hidden his pirate treasure. News of this got around, and a number of would-be fortune hunters became interested. They offered to form a company and pay Serios to guide them to Lafitte's treasure. According to Serios, Lafitte had confided that the treasure was buried in Florida.

With Serios, the expedition set off for Florida. George Johannes went along to hypnotize Serios so that he could get further instructions from Lafitte. But once in Florida, the ghost stubbornly refused to be contacted. In trance after trance Serios drew a blank. The disgusted treasure-hunting combine gave up and went home.

"Maybe Lafitte would help you take a picture of the place where he buried his treasure," Johannes suggested. He handed Serios a camera. Serios looked it over, peered into the lens, and handed it back. When the film was developed, it showed pictures of the hotel where both men had worked — hundreds of miles away in Chicago!

Perhaps it was the shock of discovering this new talent — or perhaps it was the amount of liquor Serios was now downing every day — but at this point he had a breakdown. His doctor advised him to forget about ghosts, trances, and hypnosis. His psychiatrist told him there was no such thing as photographing mental pictures.

Years went by. Now and then someone would hear about Serios, and ask him to perform. He was asked to participate in a test at the home of Curtis Fuller, an Evanston, Illinois, publisher. Fuller gave Serios a Polaroid — and Serios gave one of the most astounding demonstrations of his photographic mind!

The photo that was pulled from the test camera showed an airplane hangar. Words on the hangar made those present suspect that the hangar had something to do with the Canadian Mounted Police. Fuller sent the photo off to the Mounted Police with an inquiry.

Back came the reply: The hangar was the property of the Mounted Police. It was located in Rockcliffe, Ontario! Serios had never been to Canada. How had he managed to produce a photograph of a building he had never seen?

Dr. Eisenbud brought Ted Serios to Denver and finally managed to get a group of professors to witness a demonstration. The demonstration was a success. In one experiment, Ted was shown a magazine photo of Westminster Abbey. A few minutes later he managed to reproduce the photograph by concentrating on the Polaroid.

Dr. Eisenbud was elated — but his joy was soon turned to disappointment. He arranged for a second demonstration. Good reports had spread about Serios, and a large crowd of scientists came to observe. But Serios did not show up. He had gotten drunk and gone back to Chicago.

Unwilling to give up, Dr. Eisenbud brought Serios back to Denver, and promised the irritated spectators that Ted would appear this time. He did, but he was too drunk to talk coherently. Angered, the audience got up to leave. Suddenly Serios grabbed the camera, stared into it — and out came a sharp, clear picture of a double-decker London bus!

"Put that in your pipe and smoke it!" sneered Serios.

Serios went on to produce over one hundred mental photographs for Dr. Eisenbud. Many of them can be seen in Eisenbud's book, *The World of Ted Serios*. Some of the photos were made while Serios was blindfolded. Sometimes he used a camera from which the lens had been removed. At other times he held a plastic tube, which he called a "gismo," over the camera lens.

In spite of all these tricks, Ted Serios was able to produce both color and black-and-white photographs of buildings, cars, rockets, people, and animals.

But not all the photographs in *The World of Ted Serios* are of everyday, recognizable things. Some seem filled with weird shapes. When asked what these were, Serios would laugh. "Better ask Jean Lafitte," he would say.

The Witch's Dogs

Theriocanthropy is a tongue twister of a word. It is also a mindblower, for it means the ability of a human being to change into a lower animal.

Superstition? Probably. But in that case, how can what happened to two young men in 1871 in the English countryside be satisfactorily explained?

The young men were Michael Rendell and George French. They were medical students, headed back to classes after a Christmas holiday in the Berkshire countryside. At that time, Berkshire was a place of forests and meadows, with only a few houses or villages scattered here and there. It looked even wilder and lonelier than usual on that particular evening because a snowstorm was beginning to blot out familiar outlines.

"Medical students freeze to death in blizzard," George joked, but his laughter sounded forced. If the snow continued to thicken, they could easily lose their way. The important thing was to find shelter before the storm got worse.

"Hold up a minute!" said Michael, reigning in his horse. "There's a light up ahead. If we're lucky, it will turn out to be a hospitable farmhouse."

When they crossed through the grove, they saw that the light shone from the window of a small, weather-beaten cottage. Thankfully, they tethered their horses in a nearby shed, and knocked on the door.

The woman who opened the door was wrinkled and bent. Untidy white hair framed her head, and her smile was toothless.

"Enter, gentlemen," she said. "You may shelter here. I would not turn away dogs on a night like this!"

It was warm inside the one-room cottage — and crowded. Four large black dogs lay in front of the fireplace. A crow perched on the mantel, watching them with glittering eyes.

The old woman dipped out two bowls of broth from a steaming kettle, and handed them to the two young men.

"Eat, gentlemen," she cackled. "Who knows when you'll get broth like this again."

Slightly irritated by the old woman's habit of laughing to herself as if over some private joke, George and Michael finished their broth and lay down, sharing the fireside with the dogs. They found themselves unexpectedly drowsy and were soon fast asleep.

George awoke at dawn. He stretched, raised his arms — and was astounded to see hairy paws sticking out of his sleeves! He touched his face. It was covered with hair too! And his nose felt strange at the tip — George cried out, but the sound he made was a yelp!

An answering yelp made him turn. Now there were *five* black dogs watching him. The one that had made the sound was looking at him with Michael's eyes.

Unbelievable . . . incredible . . . These words rolled through George's dazed mind. Somehow, the old woman had turned them into huge black mastiffs. But inside their doglike heads there were still human brains, quick to seize an advantage.

The advantage came when the old woman reentered the cottage. As she opened the door, George and Michael leaped past her and ran, hampered somewhat by the shreds of human clothing that still clung to them. They loped frantically through the woods until they reached the main road. Then they stopped, their legs braced in the snow.

A man was running toward them, shouting. He wore the clothing of a priest, and carried a heavy walking stick. Thinking the dogs he saw were going to attack him, he swung the heavy stick at them.

The sunlight flashed on the silver cross on the head of the walking stick. What happened next made the priest's knees go weak so that he staggered. Instead of dogs, two frightened young men stood before him, tatters of ragged clothing flapping about their chilled bodies.

Without wasting time, the priest hurried the young men to his own house, where he steadied their nerves with brandy and a change of clothing. Then he made his way to the local authorities, where he filed a report of the incident.

"I certainly thought I saw dogs facing me on that road, vicious dogs with the torn clothing of their victims clinging to them. But then I judged I had been mistaken, for suddenly there were no dogs there — just two frightened ragged young men. They told me a terrible story of an old woman who turned them into beasts. I could have said that they had merely had a nightmare — but a nightmare would not explain the tracks in the snow!

"Coming toward me to where the young men stood were two separate sets of dog tracks. Then, only a few feet from my own tracks, the paw prints were suddenly replaced by the prints of naked human feet.

"How can one explain such things. There is not even a cottage where the young men say they sheltered — only the ruins of one. I am told that the cottage which stood there was burned down three hundred years ago. The woman who lived in it died in a fire. The old gossip in the neighborhood says that she was a witch — a woman with terrible powers!"

The Mystery of Cheiro

In a railway coach on a train speeding toward London, a young man sat reading a book on palmistry. Opposite him sat an older man with a bored expression.

As if sensing his companion's boredom, the young man closed the book and asked pleasantly: "Would you like to have me read your palm?"

With a shrug, the older man held out his hand. For a few minutes the younger man examined it carefully. Then he said: "You are a leader of men. Your dream is to see the land of your birth rule itself. You will rise to the top, but in the end your career will be broken because of a woman."

The older man looked uneasy. "That's not a very hopeful fortune. Can't you give me a better one?"

"I can't change destiny," replied the young man.

When the train pulled into London, the men exchanged cards as they said good-bye. The young man's name was Count Louis Hamon. The palm he had just read belonged to Charles Stewart Parnell, a member of Parliament, and an Irish Nationalist leader.

Did Parnell's destiny turn out as Hamon said it would? Judge for yourself. Four years later, Parnell became one of the most powerful statesman in Parliament. The Home Rule bill he had hoped for for so long was about to be introduced. Then Captain O'Shea, the husband of the woman Parnell loved, sued for divorce. The resulting scandal ruined Parnell's career — just as Hamon had foretold.

Meanwhile, Hamon was seeking his own destiny. He had gone to India and Egypt. There he studied for two years with mystics and astrologers. From them he said he learned many secrets of the occult.

With his new knowledge, Hamon returned to London. He was about to become one of the most famous men in England.

Near the rooms he rented, a man had been murdered. Scotland Yard was baffled. They knew how the man had been killed (a blow on the head with an andiron); but not why or by whom. The only clue they had was a bloody hand print on a door.

Hand prints were his specialty, so Hamon went to the scene of the crime to offer his services. The detectives yawned, but told him to go ahead and look at the print. Hamon studied it for a few minutes, then said: "The murderer is a young man. He is well-to-do, and carries a gold watch in his left trouser pocket. He is a close relative of the murdered man."

Shades of Sherlock Holmes! Reporters who were on the scene thought there might be good copy in this crazy young man. They wrote up what he had said and his face and deduction appeared in the evening papers.

The next day the reporters had another story to print about young Hamon. The police had found the killer. As Hamon had said, the murderer was young, well-to-do, carried a gold watch in his left trouser pocket — and was the son of the victim!

Now all London was talking about the mysterious young man whose prediction had solved a murder case. Hamon knew it was time to set himself up in business. He gave himself a new name — *Cheiro* (pronounced Kyro), from a Greek word meaning "hand." He set himself up as a professional palmist in a fashionable part of London.

The rich and the famous flocked to consult him. Although fortune-telling was illegal in England at the time, no one even suggested prosecuting this amazing new palmist. If he had failed to make accurate predictions, he might soon have found himself in jail. But when Cheiro the Great said something was going to happen, it happened!

On one occasion, the writer Oscar Wilde consulted Cheiro to ask him what the future held. "You will be disgraced publicly and imprisoned," replied the palmist bluntly. Three years later this prediction came true.

Lord Kitchener asked Cheiro how he would die. "You will be drowned at sea," was the answer. To prevent this from happening, Kitchener at once began to train himself to become an expert swimmer.

Cheiro also told Kitchener that he would reach a high position when he was sixty-four, which would be in 1914. When 1914 rolled around, so did World War I. Kitchener was made Commander-in-Chief of British forces. While he held this office, Kitchener often took risks that worried his subordinates. "Don't worry," he would say. "I have it on good authority that I shall die at sea."

On July 5, 1918, Kitchener was drowned when the *H.M.S. Hampshire* sank off the coast of Scotland.

King Humbert of Italy asked Cheiro what the date of his death would be. "You will die on July 29, 1900," said the palmist. On that date, the king was assassinated.

Cheiro was especially famous for a prediction he made in 1897. He was given a palm print of a Russian aristocrat to examine.

"There will be no peace for this man," said Cheiro. "He will be haunted by war and bloodshed. His end will come about twenty years from now."

The palm print belonged to Czar Nicholas II

of Russia. Twenty years later, in 1917, he and his family were murdered by Bolsheviks in a cellar.

"Until I visited Cheiro, I had no idea that the secrets of one's life were imprinted in one's hands," wrote the South African millionaire, Lionel Phillips. "Those who wish to keep their history secret should avoid an interview with Cheiro."

It was perhaps to be expected that a man as successful as Cheiro should be challenged by doubters. When he came to the United States, for example, the *New York World*, a newspaper, asked him to submit to a public test.

Cheiro accepted the challenge. The judges chose thirteen palm prints at random, and asked Cheiro to look at them and give the identity of each one.

Cheiro picked up twelve of the prints, glanced at them, and called out the correct names of their owners. When he came to the thirteenth, he turned it face down.

"I will not identify this print because it carries the mark of the murderer. He will give himself away through overconfidence, and die in prison in great misery."

As it turned out, the print did indeed belong to a murderer, Dr. Henry Meyer. He was arrested when he boasted about his crime. He died in an asylum for the criminally insane.

Cheiro's gifts served him well for a long time. He wrote a number of best sellers. He moved to Hollywood and wrote screenplays for the movies. He dreamed up a system for winning at roulette, and used it to win thousands of francs at Monte Carlo. His fortune grew and he started an investment business.

Then something went wrong. His ability to make predictions failed him. He could no longer see into the future. His own destiny was hidden from him.

Wrong decisions made matters worse. Some of his investors charged that he had mishandled their funds, and the once-great Cheiro went to prison for two years.

When he was released he found himself penniless and friendless. His once rich and powerful acquaintances would have nothing to do with him.

One morning in 1936 police found a man lying on a sidewalk in Hollywood. He was muttering incoherently, and had obviously had a stroke. He was dead when he arrived at the hospital. "His identification says he's the great Cheiro," said one of the policemen. "That's hard to believe."

It would be comforting to think that Cheiro never foresaw his own miserable end. But if he had, he would probably have said, as he said to so many others, "You cannot escape destiny."

The Killer Car

Can a machine murder? Is it possible that a car could plot and carry out crimes against people?

Sounds ridiculous, doesn't it? But if Count Franz Harrach of Serbia (now Yugoslavia) were here today, he might say: "Don't be too sure. I owned a car once — an evil, murderous machine!"

The car was a 1912 Graf and Sift, beautiful and expensive. But Count Harrach did not like to drive it. It seemed accident-prone — and the accidents always happened to people.

The Count had not forgotten the disaster of 1913 when his chauffeur was driving the car. The man always claimed that the steering wheel seemed to suddenly take on a life of its own, to twist in his hands so that the car left the road. Once the car struck down two farm workers, and then smashed into a tree. The workers had been killed, the chauffeur seriously injured — but the car was only scratched!

A few months later, a young friend of the Count's borrowed the car. On a lonely road the machine stalled. The young man got out to examine the engine. Suddenly the car lunged forward and ran over him! As a result he lost an arm.

Were these just accidents? Unhappy coincidences? The Count was beginning to wonder. He had mechanics go over it inch by inch. They could find nothing wrong. Nevertheless he locked it up and did not drive it.

A year passed. Then, in 1914, the Count received a request he could not refuse. The Archduke Francis Ferdinand, heir to the throne of Austria, asked if he and his wife might ride in the car when they toured the city of Sarajevo.

Uneasily the Count agreed. His car *was* the finest, the most luxurious car in all of Serbia — the only one fine enough to carry royalty through the capital city.

On June 28 the royal couple sat proudly in the Count's car as it rolled in the procession through Sarajebo. Suddenly a young man shoved his way through the crowd to fling a homemade bomb at the car. It landed on the car's hood.

Later some said that the bomb bounced off the car. Others said that the Archduke grabbed it and threw it out. At any rate, it exploded in the road, seriously injuring four of the Archduke's staff.

But one escape from death was all the Archduke was to be allowed. Five minutes later another assassin leaped onto the running board. His name was Gavrilo Prinzip, and he carried a gun. He fired point-blank at the royal couple, killing them both.

What followed bore out the evil reputation of the car. Because of the assassination of the royal couple, Austria declared war on Serbia. Russia took the side of Serbia, and Germany joined forces with Austria. In six weeks, all of Europe was deeply involved in World War I.

As if eager for more victims, the car itself went to war. Count Harrach, who served as an officer in the Serbian Army, used it as a staff car. But when the Count was killed in the car by an Austrian ambush, General Potiorek, Commander of the Fifty Austrian Corps, claimed the car as war booty.

Almost as soon as he stepped into the car, Potiorek's luck seemed to run downhill. In a battle a few days later, his forces were routed. Potiorek lost his command and went mad. A captain on his staff took over the automobile. Nine days later it swerved into a tree, killing him.

The war ended, and the Governor of Yugoslavia bought the car. He had it put into top condition, and drove it proudly — but not safely. In four months he had four accidents. One of them crippled him for life.

Next, another government official purchased the Graf and Sift. A few days later, while he was driving, it collided with a train. The official was killed. The car was undamaged.

"I want that machine destroyed!" demanded the Governor, who was still recuperating from his accident. "There's a curse on it."

But along came a Dr. Srkis, who didn't believe in curses. He was happy to buy the car for a fraction of its original price. But it proved to be a costly purchase. Six months later the doctor's crushed body was found beside the overturned (but only slightly damaged) car. Somehow, it had managed to roll over on him.

Next, a jeweler took over the car — and committed suicide. Then it came into the possession of a Swiss racing driver. He rebuilt the machine and souped it up. Then he entered it in the French Automobile Club race in Orleans.

At first all went well. The Swiss driver gained third place and was edging up for second. Suddenly the car swerved into a wall! The driver was thrown out and killed.

The car might have gone to a junkyard, but a well-to-do farmer took a fancy to it. He bought it and drove it peacefully for two years. Then one morning it stalled on a road. Looking for a tow, the farmer hailed a farm worker who was driving a cart.

The farmer got out and walked around the front to help tie on the tow line. Abruptly, the car's engine came to life. The machine rushed forward, running over the farmer and piling into the cart.

The last owner was still another man who didn't believe in curses. He bought the car and painted it a cheerful shade of blue. Then he invited four friends to join him for an afternoon ride. On the highway, the car went out of control and smashed into another car, killing everyone concerned.

As far as the Graf and Sift was concerned, there were no more takers. Who wanted a car that seemed to bring disaster to everyone who rode in it? It was sent to a special museum in Vienna. There, during World War II, Allied bombers finally lifted the curse by destroying the car forever.